100 GREATS
COVENTRY CITY
FOOTBALL CLUB

Dave Bennett.

100 GREATS

COVENTRY CITY
FOOTBALL CLUB

WRITTEN BY
GEORGE ROWLAND

TEMPUS

First published 2001
Copyright © George Rowland, 2001

Tempus Publishing Limited
The Mill, Brimscombe Port,
Stroud, Gloucestershire, GL5 2QG

ISBN 0 7524 2294 2

Typesetting and origination by
Tempus Publishing Limited
Printed in Great Britain by
Midway Colour Print, Wiltshire

Present and forthcoming football titles from Tempus Publishing:

Title	Format	Author	ISBN	Price
Another Day at the Office (Roger Freestone)	Pb 128pp	Keith Haynes	0 7524 2167 9	£12.99
Cambridge United FC	Images	Attmore & Nurse	0 7524 2256 1	£9.99
Charlton Athletic FC	Images	David Ramzan	0 7524 1504 2	£9.99
Crystal Palace FC	Greats	Revd Nigel Sands	0 7524 2176 X	£12.00
Everton FC 1880-1946	Images	John Rowlands	0 7524 2259 6	£10.99
Forever England	Pb 192pp	Mark Shaoul	0 7524 2042 9	£17.99
Gillingham FC	Images	Roger Triggs	0 7524 1567 0	£9.99
Gillingham FC	Players	Roger Triggs	0 7524 2243 X	£17.99
Ipswich Town FC	Images	Tony Garnett	0 7524 2152 2	£9.99
Leeds United FC	Images	David Saffer	0 7524 1642 1	£9.99
Leeds United in Europe	Images	David Saffer	0 7524 2043 7	£9.99
Leyton Orient FC	Images	Neilson Kaufman	0 7524 2094 1	£10.99
Manchester City FC	Classics	David Saffer	0 7524 2255 3	£12.00
Millwall FC 1885-1939	Images	Millwall FC Museum	0 7524 1849 1	£9.99
Queens Park Rangers FC	Images	Tony Williamson	0 7524 1604 9	£9.99
Reading FC	Greats	David Downs	0 7524 2081 X	£9.99
Reading FC 1871-1997	Images	David Downs	0 7524 1061 X	£9.99
Sniffer (Allan Clarke)	Hb 192pp	David Saffer	0 7524 2168 9	£17.99
Southend United FC	Images	Miles & Goody	0 7524 2089 5	£9.99
The Ultimate Drop	Pb 160 pp	George Rowland (Ed.)	0 7524 2217 0	£12.99
Voices of '66	Images	Norman Shiel	0 7524 2045 3	£9.99

INTRODUCTION

Compiling this record Coventry City's 100 Greats, has been a wholly enjoyable, and yet challenging task. Selecting just one hundred from the many thousands of players to have donned the colours of Coventry over the years has not been easy. Of course, there are certain players who it would have been impossible to omit – Steve Ogrizovic, George Curtis, Clarrie Bouton, George Mason – players who have contributed so much to the history of the club and whose names will forever be indelibly written in the annals of City history. Then there are the personal favourites – Ian Wallace and Mick Ferguson, Brian Borrows and Cyrille Regis – who each feature prominently in my own City memories. But then there are so many others who could have been included, and so many difficult choices to make. Someone asked me whilst I was researching this book, who would be one hundred and first in my list of Coventry City Greats, and in essence that brought home to me the subjectivity inevitably involved in this compilation. Every City fan will have their own opinion as to who are the greatest players to have played for the Sky Blues, and inevitably these opinions will differ. To try and be as objective as possible in the putting together of this book, I have endeavoured to ensure that each of the eras of Coventry history are represented: the Singers era, the Birmingham and Southern League eras, the pre-war era, the Bantams era, and of course the 'Sky Blue' era. I have also gathered the opinions of many of my fellow City fans, and tried to incorporate their views in the final selection. Whilst no collection of this type can ever be argued to constitute *the* definitive list of the one hundred greatest players in City history, I hope that all City fans enjoy reading this collection, and that any disagreement as to who has been included and those omitted leads to an enjoyable debate on the merits of City players past and present.

Coventry heroes from the 1940s and '50s, Alf Wood (left) and Peter Murphy.

ACKNOWLEDGEMENTS

Thanks must go to Jim Brown, David Brassington, Doreen Straw, Rod Dean and Coventry City Football Club for allowing the use of photographs in this book.

NOTES ON FACTUAL INFORMATION

Career Dates

The start date represents the year in which the player signed for the club, and the end date the year he was transferred or left the club. Where a player joined the club as an apprentice, the start date represents the year in which he signed professional forms, or that in which he made his first team debut, whichever was the earlier.

Appearances

Appearances as substitute are in brackets
Appearances in 'Other' column include European Fairs Cup, Full Members' (Simod, Zenith Data Systems) Cup, Texaco Cup and Charity Shield.

All efforts have been made to ensure the accuracy of factual information.

100 COVENTRY CITY GREATS

Tommy Allen
Frank Austin
Phil Babb
Jimmy Baker
Harry Barrett
Dave Bennett
Jerry Best
Jeff Blockley
Terry Bly
Jim Blyth
Brian Borrows
Clarrie Bourton
Eli Bradley
Eddie Brown
Jackie Brown
Harry Buckle
Willie Carr
Chris Cattlin
Alfred Chaplin
Dave Clements
Mick Coop
George Curtis
Gerry Daly
Jimmy Dougall
Dion Dublin
Bob Evans
Ron Farmer
Mick Ferguson
Billy Frith
Kevin Gallacher
Ian Gibson
Terry Gibson
Gary Gillespie
Bill Glazier
Bobby Gould

Micky Gynn
Mark Hateley
Frank Herbert
Brian Hill
Peter Hill
Bert Holmes
Jim Holton
Keith Houchen
Darren Huckerby
George Hudson
Willie Humphreys
Ernie Hunt
Steve Hunt
Tommy Hutchison
Leslie Jones
Eli Juggins
Mick Kearns
Brian Kilcline
Roy Kirk
Billy Lake
Jock Lauderdale
Arthur Lightening
Norman Lockhart
George Lowrie
Gary McAllister
Bobby McDonald
Martin McDonnell
Lloyd McGrath
Ken McPherson
Ernie Machin
Neil Martin
Dick Mason
George Mason
Reg Matthews
Frank Mobley

Bill Morgan
Dennis Mortimer
Peter Murphy
Peter Ndlovu
Roland Nilsson
Steve Ogrizovic
Harry Parkes
Trevor Peake
Barry Powell
Mickey Quinn
Jackie Randle
Ronnie Rees
Cyrille Regis
Brian 'Harry' Roberts
Ted Roberts
Nat Robinson
John Sillett
Noel Simpson
Billy Smith
David Speedie
Colin Stein
Ray Straw
Danny Thomas
Garry Thompson
Charlie Timmins
Ian Wallace
Leslie Warner
Alf Wood
William Yates
Terry Yorath

The top 20, who appear here in italics, occupy two pages instead of the usual one.

8

Tommy Allen
Goalkeeper, 1928-32

The turn of the 1930s was a time of free-flowing football at Highfield Road, with an attack-minded City scoring plentifully, but also conceding with distinct regularity. The custodian of the City goal at this time was Tommy Allen, a talented 'keeper who had gained an enviable reputation from his earlier service with Sunderland and Southampton. Allen faced the onerous task of presiding over the leakiest defence in City history, with the emphasis on attacking play leaving gaping holes at the back. It was Allen's performances in the City nets that often prevented their 'goals conceded' column from resembling a cricket score, and it remains somewhat of an injustice that a player who performed with such excellence in the City goal, should go down in the history books as the 'keeper to have conceded the highest number of League goals in a season, being forced to pick the ball out of his net 97 times in the 1931/32 campaign. He also had the dubious distinction of being the 'keeper responsible for conceding double figures in a League match for the only time in City's history, when a rampant Norwich City beat Coventry 10-2 in March 1930. Such records shroud the consistently excellent performances registered by Allen, which gained praise from all quarters, and made him a valued member of the side over four seasons. Born in Moxley in 1897, Allen began his playing days in local football, turning out for Wednesbury Old Athletic, Bilston United and Hickman's Institute, before being taken on by Wolverhampton Wanderers in the First World War. At the end of the war, he moved to the North-East with Sunderland, but after only a year with the Rokermen, an administrative error led to his registration with the club lapsing, and he was snapped up by Southampton in May 1920. It was whilst on the South Coast that he made the acquaintance of James McIntyre, who would later bring him to Coventry. Allen spent eight years at the Dell, during which time he made over 300 appearances and established a reputation for being a competent stopper. In June 1928, James McIntrye was appointed Coventry City's manager, and he wasted no time in bringing Allen to Highfield Road. Allen signed for City the same month and made his debut on the opening day of the 1928/29 season, keeping his first clean sheet for the club, as City beat Norwich 3-0. He was ever-present in the City side throughout his first two seasons, proving to be a model of consistency, and racking up 103 consecutive appearances. When Harry Storer became manager in June 1931, he kept faith with the City 'keeper, and Allen played throughout Storer's first full season, in which City recorded their worst defensive record ever. It was little surprise that, over the course of the next few years, Storer should place such an emphasis on establishing a consistent defence line! At the end of the 1931/32 season, after 164 appearances for City, Allen left the club to join Accrington Stanley. By now he was thirty-five, and in the twilight of his career. He stayed with Accrington for only one season before joining Northampton Town, where he made 34 League appearances in 1933/34. He continued playing non-League football with Kidderminster Harriers before retiring from the game in 1936.

| | League | | FA Cup | | Total | |
	Apps	Goals	Apps	Goals	Apps	Goals
1928/29	42	0	1	0	43	0
1929/30	42	0	4	0	46	0
1930/31	37	0	3	0	40	0
1931/32	34	0	1	0	35	0
TOTAL	155	0	9	0	164	0

Frank Austin
Wing half/Full-back, 1950-63

Only thirteen players have played for Coventry in excess of 300 times: Frank Austin is one of that elite group, making 313 appearances in thirteen years of service to City throughout the 1950s and early '60s. Born in Stoke in 1933, Austin showed promise from an early age, being selected to represent England at schoolboy level. He began his career with Toton, where he was spotted as a seventeen-year-old by the then City manager Harry Storer. After signing for City in July 1950, Austin spent three years learning the ropes in the reserves, before making his debut in April 1953 against Newport County. He became a first-team regular the following season, and proved himself to be a most consistent player. Over the next ten seasons, Austin was a fixture in the side as it struggled through one of the more difficult periods in its history.

After two years playing predominantly as a wing-half, Austin switched to a full-back role in the latter part of the 1954/55 season, proving to be equally effective in his new position. His adaptability was a significant asset to the side, and he was able to vary his play both to suit the team's needs and the style of the manager he was playing under – an important skill, given that Austin served under eight managers during his time at Highfield Road. He continued to be a regular through the dark days of the late 1950s, and up until the arrival of Jimmy Hill at the club. However, the dawn of the Sky Blue era was to prove the end of Austin's time at Highfield Road, as it soon became clear he didn't feature in Hill's plans. After playing only 26 games in the first year-and-a-half of Hill's tenure, Austin was allowed to join Torquay United in February 1963. Austin's time at Plainmoor was brief and he only made 24 League appearances for the club, before announcing his retirement from the game.

	League Apps	Goals	FA Cup Apps	Goals	League Cup Apps	Goals	Total Apps	Goals
1952/53	2	0	0	0	-	-	2	0
1953/54	37	1	1	0	-	-	38	1
1954/55	30	0	0	0	-	-	30	0
1955/56	40	0	1	0	-	-	41	0
1956/57	31	0	0	0	-	-	31	0
1957/58	33	1	1	0	-	-	34	1
1958/59	14	0	0	0	-	-	14	0
1959/60	41	0	2	0	-	-	43	0
1960/61	29	0	3	0	0	0	32	0
1961/62	37	0	2	0	1	0	40	0
1962/63	8	0	0	0	0	0	8	0
TOTAL	302	2	10	0	1	0	313	2

Phil Babb

Left-back/Centre-back, 1992-94

Phil Babb began his footballing life as a YTS trainee at Millwall, signing professional forms with the Londoners in 1988. However, two years later he was granted a free transfer and was allowed to join Bradford City in a move which kick-started his career. Babb became a regular at Valley Parade, playing as a left-back, but also featuring as a makeshift centre forward when the need arose. He impressed sufficiently in his two years with the Bantams for Bobby Gould to pay £500,000 to bring him to Highfield Road in July 1992.

He made his debut in the opening game of the 1992/93 season, featuring as a substitute in the 2-1 win over Middlesborough. His full debut came a month later in the League Cup tie with Scarborough, playing in the number 9 shirt in City's forward line. By November, however, Gould had decided that Babb's talents were best served in the defence, and he became a regular at left-back for the remainder of the season.

The following year saw Babb convert to a central defensive role, and he soon impressed with his composed and stylish brand of play. He missed only a single game during the season, his performances meriting a call-up to the Republic of Ireland squad and a full international debut in March 1994. By the latter stages of the season, Babb was creating interest throughout the Premiership and a number of offers were received for his services. His value, though, would significantly increase in the months ahead, with his exceptional performances in the World Cup in the USA.

Babb played in each of the Republic's games during the competition, and demonstrated himself able to compete with the world's finest. He helped the Irish to qualify for the second round after a famous victory over the Italians, before they bowed out to the Dutch in the second stage. By the time he arrived back in England, Babb was hot property, and a number of clubs were clamouring for his signature, with Liverpool and Spurs heading the list.

In August 1994, the inevitable happened, and with Liverpool tabling a British record bid for a defender of £3.75 million, City parted with Babb. In just two years at the Coventry, he had made 81 appearances, and increased his value by 700 per cent.

Although a regular throughout Roy Evans' time at Anfield, making 150 appearances for the Reds, Babb never fully achieved the great things that were expected of him at Liverpool. In the summer of 1999, Gerard Houllier declared Babb free to leave Anfield, and in January 2000 he spent a month on loan at First Division Tranmere Rovers. He finally left Liverpool in the summer of 2000, joining Sporting Lisbon.

	League		FA Cup		League Cup		Total	
	Apps	Goals	Apps	Goals	Apps	Goals	Apps	Goals
1992/93	27 (7)	0	1	0	2	0	30 (7)	0
1993/94	40	3	1	0	3	1	44	4
TOTAL	67 (7)	3	2	0	5	1	74 (7)	4

11

Jimmy Baker
Right half/Centre half, 1929-32 and 1933-35

Born in Trethomas in June 1904, Jimmy Baker began his playing career in his native Wales with Lovell's Athletic. His introduction to the English game didn't come until he was almost twenty-two, when he was signed by Wolverhampton Wanderers in May 1926. He spent three years at Molineux, but never established himself as a regular in the side, and was part of their reserve team when James McIntyre brought him to Highfield Road in May 1929. He slotted into the City team immediately, making his debut as a right half in the opening day fixture of 1929/30 against Merthyr Town. He played the majority of his 27 matches during this season as a wing-half; however, midway through the following year, he converted to centre half, a position he played predominantly over the following two seasons.

Unmistakable due to his flame-red hair, Baker was a consistent and reliable performer for the City side of the late 1920s and early '30s. He missed relatively few matches, registering as an ever-present in 1930/31. In the close season of 1932, Baker shocked City by returning to Lovell's Athletic, although after a mere eight months he was back at Highfield Road, and thrust back into Harry Storer's side, once again as right half. He continued as first choice in the number 4 shirt until midway through the 1934/35 season, when competition from the emerging Billy Frith ousted him for a significant part of the campaign. By this stage, Storer was clearly looking to the future and was keen to allow Frith the opportunity to develop in the first team. Realizing that his place in the side was under serious threat, Baker chose to move on in the close season of 1935, joining Bristol City. His move to Ashton Gate did not prove to be a success and, in his two seasons with Bristol, he played only 11 matches. In the summer of 1937, he made his final move joining the fledgling Colchester United side – who had only been formed months earlier. He remained with the U's until midway through the Second World War, when, approaching forty, he retired from the game.

	League		FA Cup		Total	
	Apps	Goals	Apps	Goals	Apps	Goals
1929/30	27	3	0	0	27	3
1930/31	42	4	3	0	45	4
1931/32	39	1	2	0	41	1
1932/33	8	1	0	0	8	1
1933/34	39	2	2	0	41	2
1934/35	27	0	0	0	27	0
TOTAL	182	11	7	0	189	11

Harry Barrett
Wing-half 1934-52

Harry Barrett joined City as a fresh-faced sixteen-year-old in 1934, signing from works side, Alfred Herbert's Athletic. It was the start of almost twenty years at City, during which time he made over 175 first-class appearances, not including a significant number during the war. Barrett served his apprenticeship in the reserve side during his early years at City, and also had a spell on loan at Cheltenham Town to gain further experience. It was not until 1938 that he made his first-team debut, in one of only a handful of matches he played during the pre-war era.

It was during the war itself that Barrett made the progression to first-team football, turning out 110 times for the wartime side, as well as guesting for Leicester City. Once peacetime football resumed, he became a regular in the first team, where he remained for five full seasons. Barrett was immensely versatile and, although naturally a wing-half, he could adapt to play wherever necessary. Indeed, during his time with City, he turned out in no fewer than nine positions, including a twenty-minute spell in goal for the injured Alf Wood.

During his final full season at City, Barrett was club captain, a position he relished. His career came to an end following a knee injury sustained in the opening match of the 1951/52 season. After his retirement, he went on to manage Rugby Town and, later, Snowdon Colliery, where he discovered future City stars George Curtis, Eric Jones, and Alf Bentley. He returned to City for a brief spell as chief scout in 1955, before going on to manage Gillingham between 1957 and 1962.

	League		FA Cup		Total	
	Apps	Goals	Apps	Goals	Apps	Goals
1937/38	1	0	0	0	1	0
1938/39	4	1	0	0	4	1
1945/46	-	-	2	1	2	1
1946/47	33	7	2	0	35	7
1947/48	38	0	2	0	40	0
1948/49	37	0	1	0	38	0
1949/50	26	2	0	0	26	2
1950/51	30	2	1	0	31	2
1951/52	1	0	0	0	1	0
TOTAL	170	12	8	1	178	13

Dave Bennett

Outside right, 1983-89

Dave Bennett was a true fans' favourite at City, his delightful skill and mastery on the right wing creating a host of opportunities for Big Cyrille and others during the exciting days of the late 1980s. He is perhaps best remembered for his performances in the 1987 Cup run – his cross for the equalising goal at Hillsborough in the semi-final, followed by his injury time winner sent thousands of City fans into delirium. In the final itself, Bennett showed his class, sidestepping Spurs 'keeper Ray Clemence to net the first equaliser. Then, in the second half it was from Bennett's cross that Keith Houchen scored his famous diving header to take the match into extra-time. It is a testament to Bennett that, on his return to Highfield Road after his move to Sheffield Wednesday, he received a reception which matches any for a returning former player.

Bennett began his career with Manchester City, signing as a professional in June 1977. In his four years at Maine Road, he made 52 appearances and was part of the 1981 Cup Final team. In September of 1981 he signed for Cardiff City, joining up with his brother, Gary, and two years later was brought to Coventry by Bobby Gould in a deal worth £100,000.

He made his debut in the home win over Leicester in September 1983 and was a regular throughout his first season at City, weighing in with 7 goals. However, in his early seasons at City he never truly fulfilled his promise and was at times frustrating with occasional glimpses of brilliance shrouded by often very average performances. It was not until the era of Curtis and Sillett that Bennett began truly expressing himself and demonstrated his deft skills on a regular basis.

He remained at Coventry until March of 1989, making 209 appearances for the Sky Blues, before transferring to Sheffield Wednesday for £250,000. After a year and only 30 appearances for the Hillsborough club, he moved on to Swindon Town, where suffered a most unfortunate string of injuries. In only his second game, Bennett broke his leg, keeping him out of action for the best part of a year. As part of his rehabilitation he was loaned out to Shrewsbury Town, but broke the same leg in his second game for his loan club. Eight months later, whilst in pre-season training back at Swindon, he again suffered a broken leg. He retired from first-class football shortly afterwards, dropping into the non-League game as player-coach with Atherstone United.

	League		FA Cup		League Cup		Other		Total	
	Apps	Goals	Apps	Goals	Apps	Goals	Apps	Goals	Apps	Goals
1983/84	32 (2)	6	3	0	3	1	0	0	38 (2)	7
1984/85	29 (5)	2	0	0	2	0	0	0	31 (5)	2
1985/86	33 (5)	6	1	0	4	2	2	0	40 (5)	8
1986/87	31	7	5	3	5	2	1	0	42	12
1987/88	27 (1)	4	2	0	3	0	4	2	36 (1)	6
1988/89	5 (2)	0	1	0	0	0	1	0	7 (2)	0
TOTAL	157(15)	25	12	3	17	5	8	2	194(15)	35

Jerry Best
Goalkeeper, 1920-26

Undoubtedly, Jerry Best's performances in City's goal during the early 1920s saved them from some very heavy defeats, as the team struggled in their first years as a League club. He was an unlikely figure for a custodian, and at only 5ft 7in, he registers as City's shortest ever League 'keeper. During the First World War, he was shot in the arm and carried a noticeable injury, but this never detracted from his performances. He signed for City from the Mickley Colliery Club in May 1920, making his debut in the Christmas Day match of the same year, which City lost 4-2 to Cardiff City. Two days later, in the return leg at Ninian Park, his heroics kept out all that promotion-chasing Cardiff could throw at him, as City recorded a surprise 1-0 victory.

From Christmas 1920, Best was City's regular goalkeeper for six seasons, missing only 9 matches during this time. Between November 1921 and December 1925, Best played in 180 consecutive League and Cup matches for City, and became the first City player to record over 200 League appearances for the club. In November 1925, he became the first player to be awarded a testimonial for League service, in what would be his final season with the club.

At the end of the 1925/26 season, City were in severe financial trouble. As a cost-cutting measure, they offered all their players reduced wages, an offer refused by their star 'keeper. He left Highfield Road at the start of the following season, joining Halifax Town. He remained at the Shay for only one campaign, making 9 appearances before moving to Yorkshire rivals, Rotherham United. Again, his stay with Rotherham was only for a single season, the 26 League games he played for them proving to be his last in the League. In the close season of 1929, Best dropped into non-League football with Worksop Town. After a brief spell with Newark Town in the early 1930s, Best returned to Worksop, where he saw out his playing days.

	League		FA Cup		Total	
	Apps	Goals	Apps	Goals	Apps	Goals
1920/21	23	0	2	0	25	0
1921/22	40	0	3	0	43	0
1922/23	42	0	1	0	43	0
1923/24	42	0	2	0	44	0
1924/25	42	0	3	0	45	0
1925/26	35	0	1	0	36	0
TOTAL	224	0	12	0	236	0

Jeff Blockley

Centre half, 1967-72

Coventry emerged from the 1960s with the most promising crop of young talent for many years. During the late 1960s and early '70s, players of the calibre of Willie Carr, Dennis Mortimer, and Alan Green graduated from the youth scheme, to serve City with excellence, well into the 1970s. Perhaps the finest youth side of this period was that which reached the FA Youth Cup final in 1968, captained by a centre half named Jeff Blockley. Blockley was an uncompromising defender, who showed maturity beyond his years and a natural affinity for leading the defence. It was no surprise when he was promoted to the first team aged just nineteen, making his debut as a substitute in the 1-0 defeat against Southampton in January 1969.

Blockley's performances in the first team created a storm of excitement, as he made the transition to First Division football effortlessly. He quickly established himself as a regular in the heart of the City defence and, from the start of the 1969/70 campaign, missed only 5 matches in three seasons. His promise was rewarded with a call-up to the England under-23 team in 1971, for whom he made 6 appearances whilst a Sky Blue. He also represented the Football League XI in the game against the Scottish League in 1972 and was called up to the full England squad later the same year. Although his call-up came whilst he was still a City player, his international debut came just two days after his transfer to Arsenal in October 1972, robbing City of their first full England player since Reg Matthews.

The arrival of Gordon Milne as City's manager marked the end of Blockley's time at City, and a £200,000 offer from Arsenal was sufficient to tempt Milne to dispense with the central defender. The move was not a success for Blockley, who was never a regular at Highbury and made just 62 appearances in three years. In January 1975, he left London to join his home-town club of Leicester City for a fee of £100,000. He remained at Filbert Street for three years, before a spell on loan at Derby preceded a move to Notts County in June 1978. Blockley's League career came to an end in 1980 when, after leaving Meadow Lane, he dropped into the non-League game with Gloucester City.

	League		FA Cup		League Cup		Other		Total	
	Apps	Goals	Apps	Goals	Apps	Goals	Apps	Goals	Apps	Goals
1968/69	10 (2)	0	0	0	0	0	0	0	10 (2)	0
1969/70	39	3	1	0	1	0	0	0	41	3
1970/71	42	1	1	0	5	1	4	1	52	3
1971/72	42	2	1	0	1	0	4	2	48	4
1972/73	11	0	0	0	1	0	2	0	14	0
TOTAL	144 (2)	6	3	0	8	1	10	3	165 (2)	10

Terry Bly

Centre forward, 1962-63

When news broke of Terry Bly's sale to Notts County in August 1963, there was an outcry from the fans. Bly had been with the club for only one season, but in that short time, he had dazzled with his attacking flair and goalscoring. It was the dawn of the Sky Blue era, and with Bly seemingly the jewel in the Sky Blue crown, it seemed tantamount to lunacy to allow him to depart. Jimmy Hill, however, thought otherwise, and, although Bly's replacement, George Hudson, proved to be just as dynamic a performer, this did little to placate the angry City fans in the summer of 1963.

Bly had come to City as a £10,000 signing from Peterborough in July 1962. His reputation as a clinical marksman preceded him, after netting 54 goals, a Fourth Division record, in his final season with the Posh. A scoring debut in the opening game of the 1963/64 season against Notts County, was followed by a hat-trick a fortnight later against Southend, setting the tone for the season. In mid-October, Bly embarked on a scoring run which saw him net 17 times in 16 League games, including a run of 7 consecutive scoring League matches. At the end of this phenomenal run, Bly was surprisingly dropped in favour of the newly-arrived Hudson. He played only a single further match, again scoring as City drew with Bristol Rovers in April, and left in the close season. In all, Bly had scored 30 in 42 games in his solitary year with the Sky Blues.

With hindsight, Hill's decision to dispense with Bly's services proved shrewd. The £13,000 received from Notts County was a tidy sum, and once at Meadow Lane, the goals dried up. He remained for only one season before dropping into non-League football as Grantham Town's player-manager. Bly ended up staying with Grantham for fifteen years, before leaving the game.

	League		FA Cup		League Cup			Total	
	Apps	Goals	Apps	Goals	Apps	Goals		Apps	Goals
1962/63	32	26	8	3	2	1		42	30
TOTAL	32	26	8	3	2	1		42	30

Jim Blyth
Goalkeeper, 1972-82

Jim Blyth signed for City from Preston North End as a promising seventeen-year-old in October 1972. His fee was £22,000, which eventually rose to £40,000 with extra payments as Blyth graduated to the first-team and eventually won international honours. For his first three seasons at City, Blyth understudied first Bill Glazier and then Bryan King. His opportunity came in late 1975 when King suffered an injury and Blyth was promoted to the first team. Over the next seven seasons at City, Blyth played regularly, developing into an excellent 'keeper, who could have achieved much more had it not been for an unfortunate back injury.

Blyth made his debut in December 1975, in the 2-1 defeat against Everton, and over the course of the 1975/76 campaign, established himself as City's first-choice custodian. He developed over the next two seasons, enjoying fine form, which was already attracting the attention of both Scotland manager Ally McLeod and other First Division clubs. 1977/78 proved to be the zenith of his career as he excelled in the successful City side which narrowly missed out on European qualification. It also marked the start of his international career, the first of his two full Scotland caps coming in the 2-1 win over Bulgaria in February 1978. At the end of the season he travelled as part of the Scotland World Cup squad to Argentina, but never featured as Scotland bade an early farewell to the finals with a first-round exit.

Towards the end of 1978, Blyth sustained a back injury, which proved a major factor in his remaining career. In November of the same year, his back trouble prevented a move to Old Trafford, when Manchester United agreed a £440,000 fee, only for the deal to break down at the medical. It also allowed a young Les Sealey to get his break in the first-team, and for the remainder of Blyth's time at Highfield Road, he was forced to share the goalkeeping duties with his young rival.

After an elongated spell in the first-team at the start of the 1981/82 season, Blyth was dropped for the final time after a disappointing display in the FA Cup exit to West Brom. In the close season he moved on to Birmingham City on a free transfer. His time at St Andrews was spent acting as understudy to Tony Coton and the emerging David Seaman and, after two years and just 14 appearances for the Blues, he left to join non-League Nuneaton Borough, where he finished his playing career in 1986.

	League		FA Cup		League Cup		Total	
	Apps	Goals	Apps	Goals	Apps	Goals	Apps	Goals
1975/76	19	0	1	0	0	0	20	0
1976/77	31	0	2	0	3	0	36	0
1977/78	40	0	0	0	4	0	44	0
1978/79	6	0	2	0	0	0	8	0
1979/80	21	0	1	0	1	0	23	0
1980/81	7	0	0	0	3	0	10	0
1981/82	27	0	4	0	2	0	33	0
TOTAL	151	0	10	0	13	0	174	0

Brian Borrows
Right-back, 1985-97

If Coventry City were to initiate an award for the most unfortunate player in their history, then the name of Brian Borrows would have to be high on the list of candidates for that dubious honour. After missing only one game in the exciting 1986/87 season, and playing in each round of the FA Cup run, 'Bugsy' sustained a knee injury in the final League game of the season, and was robbed of a place in the FA Cup final side a week later. Whilst Sillett led the players onto the Wembley turf, Borrows was forced to watch proceedings from a hospital bed. The subsequent victory and honorary winners' medal awarded to Borrows was small consolation for missing what was to be his only opportunity to play in a major final.

Borrows signed for Coventry in June 1985, a bargain buy from Bolton at £80,000. He had begun his career at Everton, but was limited to just 29 appearances in three years at Goodison, due to the competition he faced for the right-back place from future England player, Gary Stevens. He moved to Bolton in 1983 and made 106 appearances for the Trotters, before Don MacKay brought him to Highfield Road. He immediately slotted in to the right-back position, that had never been adequately filled since the departure of Danny Thomas in 1983.

Borrows was a stylish full-back, who was one of City's most consistent and talented performers during the late 1980s and early '90s. He was touted for international honours, but was overlooked by successive England managers, his only representative call-up being for a 'B' international against Czechoslovakia in 1990. In the same year, he was voted the club's Player of the Year, an award he won for a second time in 1994/95. In his twelve years at City, he amassed 488 League and Cup appearances, a total only bettered by Ogrizovic, Coop and Curtis.

Bugsy eventually left Coventry in the summer of 1997, joining Swindon Town on a free transfer, after a period on loan with the Wiltshire club.

	League		FA Cup		League Cup		Other		Total	
	Apps	Goals	Apps	Goals	Apps	Goals	Apps	Goals	Apps	Goals
1985/86	41	0	1	0	4	0	2	0	48	0
1986/87	41	1	5	0	5	0	1	0	52	1
1987/88	32 (1)	0	2	0	3	0	3 (1)	0	40 (2)	0
1988/89	38	1	1	0	3	0	1	0	43	1
1989/90	37	1	1	0	8	0	1	0	47	1
1990/91	38	6	4	0	5	0	1	0	48	6
1991/92	34 (1)	0	2	1	3	0	1	0	40 (1)	1
1992/93	36 (2)	2	1	0	2	1	0	0	39 (2)	3
1993/94	29	0	1	0	1	0	0	0	31	0
1994/95	33 (2)	0	4	0	1	0	0	0	38 (2)	0
1995/96	21	0	1	0	3	0	0	0	25	0
1996/97	16 (7)	0	3	0	4	0	0	0	23 (7)	0
TOTAL	396(13)	11	26	1	42	1	10(1)	0	474(14)	13

Clarrie Bourton

Forward, 1931-37

In terms of goalscoring, Clarrie Bourton was, undoubtedly, City's greatest ever player. His record of 180 goals for Coventry remains unsurpassed, and perhaps what is even more impressive, is that it was achieved in only 241 games. Bourton also holds the record for goals scored in a season for City, his tally of 50 in 1931/2 (49 of them in the League) being achieved in his first season for the club.

Bourton was born on 30 September 1908 in Bristol, and began his football career at Bristol City, signing shortly before the start of the 1927/28 campaign. After only 4 appearances, however, he transferred to Ewood Park, in a combined deal worth £3,650 (Albert Keating being the player transferred with Bourton). In his three years at Blackburn, he played a total of 63 games, netting 37 goals for the Lancashire team. It was this striking prowess that attracted the attention of Harry Storer, and in April 1931 he signed for City for a mere £750. Bourton was an instant success and in his first season at the club, he topped the League goalscoring charts. His 49 goals that campaign included 5 hat-tricks, one four and one five-goal haul. Bourton continued his goalscoring exploits the following season, again ably supported by fellow City greats, Jock Lauderdale and Billy Lake. It was the Bourton era which established the terrace chant 'Come on the Old Five', in reference to the regularity with which Coventry put five goals past the opposition. Bourton scored 38 League goals in 1932/33, a total only surpassed by Hull City's Ken McNaughton.

He continued scoring regularly over the next three seasons, and was a key figure in the Third Division (South) championship-winning team of 1935/36. However, he found the transition to Second Division football difficult and the goals began to dry up, with only 9 in City's first season back in the second level of the Football League. In October 1937, Bourton left Highfield Road for Plymouth Argyle, but, unable to settle at Home Park, he soon returned to his home town of Bristol, first as a player, and then as manager of Bristol City. Finally hanging up his boots in 1944, Bourton remained with the Robins in various capacities, until his death in 1981 (by which time he worked the club's pool office).

In his six full seasons at Highfield Road, Bourton scored an unsurpassed 13 hat-tricks in a side which averaged over 90 goals a season. Little wonder that the early 1930s are remembered as the 'glory days' for Coventry City.

	League		FA Cup		Total	
	Apps	Goals	Apps	Goals	Apps	Goals
1931/32	40	49	2	1	42	50
1932/33	39	38	4	3	43	41
1933/34	30	25	2	0	32	25
1934/35	39	26	3	3	42	29
1935/36	39	24	2	2	41	26
1936/37	36	9	0	0	36	9
1937/38	5	0	0	0	5	0
TOTAL	228	171	13	9	241	180

Clarrie Bourton – a goal machine in the 1930s.

Eli Bradley
Centre half, 1909-1912

Eli Bradley was one of Coventry City's most outstanding performers during the Southern League era. Operating at centre half, he was renowned as a tough-tackling, robust defender, who provided City with strength and stability at the back over four seasons. Born in 1882, he began his career as a sixteen-year-old with local side Bilston Town. Whilst at Bilston, he earned his only international honours, representing the England youth side against Scotland in 1899. After a spell with Dudley, he signed for West Brom in July 1905.

At the Hawthorns, Bradley played in a variety of positions, including centre forward and outside right, demonstrating his versatility with excellent performances in whatever role he was asked to play. He moved on to Luton Town in 1908, where he continued to operate as a utility player, and, indeed, played against Coventry as a centre forward in 1908/09. In the summer of 1909, he moved to Highfield Road. Throughout his time at City, Bradley played at centre half, a position he was known to favour. He was not averse, however, to pressing forward and became renowned for his powerful long-range shots, known amongst the fans as 'Eli's pile-drivers'. His attacking forays produced 20 goals in his four years at City, his best haul coming in 1910/11, when he registered 10 League strikes.

By 1911, Bradley's performances were attracting the attentions of City's rivals. A substantial offer for his services came in from Oldham Athletic, but was rebuffed by City with Bradley's backing, stating that he was happy to remain at Highfield Road. League representative selectors had also taken note of his talents, and he played in each of the three inter-League matches in 1911/12.

Bradley's career at Coventry ended on a sour note the following season. Whilst carrying an injury, Bradley received barracking from City fans during the 3-2 home defeat against Merthyr Tydfil. Taking offence at his treatment, he requested a transfer and it was to be the last game he played for the club. In October 1912, he signed for Scottish side Hearts for a fee of £500, after 116 games for Coventry.

After impressing in his early performances north of the Border, Bradley sustained a serious knee injury and was forced to retire from first-class football at the end of his first season with Hearts. He returned to his native Dudley, where he rejoined Dudley Town, continuing to play at this level for a further six years. He finally retired from the game completely in 1919.

| | Southern League | | FA Cup | | Total | |
	Apps	Goals	Apps	Goals	Apps	Goals
1909/10	37	4	6	1	43	5
1910/11	33	10	4	0	37	10
1911/12	27	4	2	0	29	4
1912/13	7	1	0	0	7	1
TOTAL	104	19	12	1	116	20

Eddie Brown
Centre forward, 1952-54

Eddie Brown arrived at Highfield Road with City in the midst of a dire relegation battle late on in the 1951/52 season. His signing was a last-ditch attempt by Harry Storer to pull City clear of danger, but in reality little could be done to preserve Coventry's precarious status in the Second Division. Brown duly contributed three strikes in the last nine games of the season, but it was to prove too little to avoid the drop to the Third. Over the next two seasons, Brown proved to be an excellent acquisition, spurring on the team's attack with his electrifying pace and prolific scoring. During his two-year stay at City, he notched 51 goals in 89 games, and became a real favourite with the fans. His departure during a poor run of form in 1954 was greeted with disapproval from the City masses, but was indicative of a time at Coventry where 'crisis' management consisted of repeatedly trying to find short-term fixes to inherent problems. Such moves would be repeated throughout the 1950s, as City struggled to find any stability either on or off the field and embarked one of the darkest periods of their history.

By the time he came to City, Brown had already earned a name for himself as a striker of some repute, enjoying an excellent scoring record wherever he played. His career began in 1948 with Preston North End, where he played 31 League games, scoring 14 times. In 1950 he moved on to Southampton, where he top-scored in his debut campaign with 20 League strikes. Midway through his second year at the Dell he requested a transfer and signed for City in a deal worth £7,000. For both of his two full seasons with Coventry, Brown was the club's top-scorer, netting 19 and 20 goals respectively. His bustling style of play was well suited to the Third Division, and he was a fixture in the forward line as City strove for a quick return to the Second. He started the 1954/55 season in a similar vein, with nine goals in the first eight games, but there then followed a mini-crisis that would spell the end of his time at Highfield Road. In the next six matches, City lost four and drew two, with Brown failing to score. The club announced that 'drastic changes' were needed, and concluded that Brown should be sold. The more sceptical of supporters viewed his sale as motivated by financial rather than playing reasons; however, the outcome either way was that Brown was sold to Birmingham City in October 1954.

Brown continued to flourish at St Andrews, averaging just under a goal every other game throughout his four-year stay. He helped the side to the FA Cup final of 1956, and also playing in each of the first four seasons of the European Fairs Cup between 1955 and 1958. He moved on to Leyton Orient in 1959, where he played his final two years of League football. By the time he dropped into the non-League game with Scarborough in 1961, he had scored 190 League goals in just under 400 games. He went on to play for a number of non-League sides, including Stourbridge, Bedworth Town and Wigan Athletic, before retiring as a player and becoming a teacher.

	League		FA Cup		Total	
	Apps	Goals	Apps	Goals	Apps	Goals
1951/52	9	3	0	0	9	3
1952/53	31	18	3	1	34	19
1953/54	33	20	1	0	34	20
1954/55	12	9	0	0	12	9
TOTAL	85	50	4	1	89	51

Jackie Brown

Outside right, 1936-38

Jackie Brown signed for Coventry at the height of the Harry Storer era, in the mid-1930s. City had just won promotion to the Second Division, but early on in their return to Division Two, regular outside right, George McNestry, suffered an ankle injury. When it became apparent that McNestry would be out for some time, Storer turned to Brown, drafting him in from Wolverhampton Wanderers for £3,000. He proved to be a more than adequate replacement and, over the next two seasons, he served the City forward line excellently – proving not only to be a stylish winger, but also a goalscorer of some repute.

Brown's playing days had begun in his native Belfast where, in his teens, he had played for Belfast Celtic. His performances in Ireland had been noted by a number of English clubs and, in late 1934, Major Frank Buckley brought him across the Irish Channel to Wolves. In two years at Molineux, he vied for the right wing position with George Ashall, making 31 appearances and scoring 7 goals, before joining City in October 1936. He settled into the City side immediately, and by the end of his first season at the club, he was the team's top scorer with 14 goals. In 1937, he gained the distinction of becoming Coventry's only dual international, representing the Republic of Ireland, having already won 4 caps for the Northern Irish team while at Highfield Road.

Brown's second, and final, season at City saw him continuing the rich vein of form that had served the club so well in his first. He was, once again, top scorer, netting 15 as City pushed to their highest ever pre-war finish of fourth in the Second Division. However, in September of 1938, Brown was involved in what was described as an 'unfortunate incident' in a Coventry ballroom, and it was this off-the-field incident that would precipitate his premature departure from Highfield Road. He was sold to Birmingham City in the same month, and was part of the Blues team that was relegated to the Second Division in 1939.

After the Second World War had interrupted his career, Brown enjoyed something of an Indian summer in the late 1940s. After spending the immediate post-war years playing non-League football with Barry Town, he was signed by Ipswich in 1948, at the age of thirty-three. He remained at Ipswich for three years, making 103 appearances and scoring 27 goals, before finally retiring as a player in 1951.

	League		FA Cup		Total	
	Apps	Goals	Apps	Goals	Apps	Goals
1936/37	29	13	3	1	32	14
1937/38	40	13	1	2	41	15
TOTAL	69	26	4	3	73	29

Harry Buckle
Outside left, 1908-11

Born in Belfast in 1882, Harry Buckle began his football career with Irish sides Cliftonville Casuals and Cliftonville Olympic, before crossing the Irish Sea to join First Division Sunderland in 1902. He spent four years at Roker Park, making 46 appearances and scoring 15 goals for the Wearsiders. It was during his spell in the North-East that Buckle gained the first of his two international caps for Ireland, featuring in the 3-1 defeat at the hands of England in Belfast in 1904. It would be a further four years before his second and final cap, and, despite the fact that he never appeared for his national team whilst at Highfield Road, this made him one of only a handful of full international players to have turned out for Coventry up until this time.

From Sunderland, Buckle moved south to join Portsmouth in May 1906. He remained at Fratton Park for a solitary season, making 15 Southern League appearances and netting 3 goals. From Pompey, Buckle transferred to Bristol Rovers in the close season of 1907, where he spent one season before joining Coventry in 1908.

Buckle's arrival at Highfield Road co-incided with their election to the Southern League, and his first campaign at the club was spent in a side struggling to make their mark at the higher level. He made his debut in the opening day clash with Crystal Palace, and missed only one game throughout the season, providing the side with much-needed class and attacking drive from the left-flank. He top scored for City in his first season, his tally of 17 goals including a hat-trick in the 5-3 win over Portsmouth, and three 'braces' against Southend, Queens Park Rangers and Leyton.

Prior to the start of the 1909/10 season, Buckle was given the responsibility of team manager as well as continuing as a player. Again he finished the campaign as top scorer, with nineteen strikes, and led the club to the quarter-finals of the FA Cup, a run which included famous victories over First Division opponents Preston North End and Nottingham Forest. He remained a first-team regular during his third and final season with the club, during which he netted his second and final hat-trick in the 5-1 win over Southend. In the summer of 1911, after three years and 126 appearances at Highfield Road, he returned to Ireland to join Belfast Celtic as player/manager.

Once back in Ireland, Buckle supplemented his income in the Belfast shipyards, where he was one of only seventeen Catholics employed. With religious friction rife, Buckle found himself at the brunt of a number of unpleasant incidents due to his faith, having an iron bolt fired in his face on one occasion, and ending up being thrown in the Belfast Lough on a second. On the field, he remained with the Celtic side for three seasons before joining Glenarvon in 1914, and Belfast United in 1917, again combining his playing duties with the role of manager, and indeed secretary whilst with United.

At the age of forty, Buckle made his final move, joining Cork side Fordson's in 1922. He continued playing until well into his forties, and enjoyed an Indian Summer with two Irish Cup final appearances to mark the close of his career. After the cup success of 1926, Buckle finally retired, after a career which had spanned almost thirty years.

	Southern League		FA Cup			Total	
	Apps	Goals	Apps	Goals		Apps	Goals
1908/09	39	17	3	0		42	17
1909/10	38	17	6	2		44	19
1910/11	36	9	4	1		40	10
TOTAL	**113**	**43**	**13**	**3**		**126**	**46**

Coventry City 1909/10. From left to right, back row: E. Kinnear (trainer), W. Hickleton, P. Saul, R. Evans, E. Bradley, W. Hanson, A. Chaplin. Front row: C. Tickle, G. Warren, W. Smith, E. Hendren, H. Buckle.

Willie Carr
Midfield, 1967-75

Carr was a home-grown talent, progressing through the youth ranks into the first-team, where he remained for eight seasons in the late 1960s and early '70s. He made his full debut whilst still in the youth team, injury necessitating his selection against Southampton in September 1967, while he was still only seventeen. Carr acquitted himself well in his early performances, and from February of the 1967/68, he became a regular in the starting line up. His explosive pace and natural passing ability made him a danger to even the best opposition, and he was regularly the instrument of goalscoring moves and striking opportunities. Although never prolific, Carr also weighed in with 37 goals during his time at City. His most memorable moment whilst at City, undoubtedly came in October 1970 when he 'teed up' Ernie Hunt for the infamous donkey kick goal against Everton. The move saw Carr stand astride the ball at an attacking free-kick, before flicking the ball backwards and into the air with his heels. This allowed Ernie Hunt to spectacularly volley the ball over the wall and past Andy Rankin in the Everton net. The move was later outlawed by FIFA, who decreed that it contravened the law regarding the ball moving its full circumference from a free-kick. However, this was not until it had earned Carr and Hunt the 'Goal of the Season' award, and a place in City folklore.

1970 also saw Carr win his first full international caps, having already represented Scotland at both youth and under-23 levels. He made his debut in the 1-0 victory over Northern Ireland in April, and went on to play for his country six times before sustaining a major knee injury in City's match with Liverpool in 1973. The injury not only kept him out of domestic football for eight months, but also brought his international career to a premature end, at a time when he seemed a virtual certainty to be part of the squad for the 1974 World Cup finals.

Carr returned from injury in late 1973, and in the following year looked set for a transfer to Wolves when City accepted a bid of £240,000 for his services. The move, however, fell through on medical grounds and Carr remained at Highfield Road for a further season. Wolves eventually got their man in March 1975, for the significantly reduced price of £100,000, and Carr went on to make over 200 appearances for the Molineux club. He ended his career with a short spell at Millwall, before dropping into non-League football with Worcester City in February 1983.

	League		FA Cup		League Cup		Other		Total	
	Apps	Goals	Apps	Goals	Apps	Goals	Apps	Goals	Apps	Goals
1967/68	20 (3)	1	3	1	0 (1)	0	0	0	23 (4)	2
1968/69	33 (3)	3	2	0	3	0	0	0	38 (3)	3
1969/70	38	4	2	0	1	0	0	0	41	4
1970/71	41	5	1	0	5	1	4	0	51	6
1971/72	42	8	2	0	1	0	4	0	49	8
1972/73	36	8	3	1	2	1	2	0	43	10
1973/74	12 (1)	1	5	0	1	0	0	0	18 (1)	1
1974/75	23	3	3	0	1	0	0	0	27	3
TOTAL	245 (7)	33	21	2	14 (1)	2	10	0	290 (8)	37

Chris Cattlin
Left-back, 1968-76

Chris Cattlin was so popular with the Sky Blue faithful, that when news broke of the club's intention to grant him a free transfer in 1976, a petition was gathered urging a rethink. Alas, it was to no avail, and 'Spider', as he had become known, was to depart for Brighton, after eight years' excellent service to Coventry. When he signed for City in March 1968, the fee of £70,000 represented a British record for a left-back, a sum he justified almost immediately in the newly-promoted City side, which was struggling to maintain their First Division status. His performances in City's defence helped the club maintain and consolidate their top-flight position, and progress into their only European campaign to date, in 1970/71. By the time he left Highfield Road, he had established himself as one of the foremost defenders in City's top-flight history.

Cattlin's City career began with the daunting task of marking a certain George Best, on the occasion of Manchester United's first League visit to Highfield Road in a First Division fixture in March 1968 – a task he performed immaculately, as City defeated the Reds, 2-0. For the remainder of the season, Cattlin played a vital role in City's successful battle against relegation, and helped the club guarantee survival with a point in their final fixture at Southampton. The following year, his performances earned him a call-up to the England under-23 squad, making his debut against Wales in 1968. He made a second under-23 appearance in the same year, but he did not progress any further in international football, despite his continued consistent performances in City's defence.

Over the course of his eight years at City, Cattlin made 239 appearances in all competitions. A year after he left to join Brighton, Coventry honoured his service to the Sky Blues by sending a side to the South Coast for a testimonial fixture, a fitting tribute to a player many felt had been treated badly by the club in the manner of his departure. He remained at the Goldstone Ground for four years, before retiring as a player in 1980, returning in 1983 for a three-year spell as the Seagulls' manager. Upon his dismissal in 1986, he remained in Brighton and established a 'rock' shop on the seafront, perhaps the furthest removed of occupations from football!

	League		FA Cup		League Cup		Other		Total	
	Apps	Goals	Apps	Goals	Apps	Goals	Apps	Goals	Apps	Goals
1967/68	11	0	0	0	0	0	0	0	11	0
1968/69	32(1)	0	2	0	3	0	0	0	37(1)	0
1969/70	32(1)	0	1	0	1	0	0	0	32(1)	0
1970/71	14(1)	0	0	0	0	0	1	0	15(1)	0
1971/72	29	0	2	0	0	0	1	0	32	0
1972/73	36	0	2	0	2	0	1	0	41	0
1973/74	5(1)	0	1	0	0(1)	0	0	0	6(2)	0
1974/75	400	0	3	0	1	0	0	0	44	0
1975/76	140	0	0	0	0	0	0	0	14	0
TOTAL	213(4)	0	11	0	7(1)	0	3	0	234(5)	0

Alfred Chaplin
Wing half, 1902-03 & 1906-12

Born in Foleshill in 1879, Alfred Chaplin began playing football with local sides St Pauls and Great Heath. At this time he usually operated as a wing-half; however, whilst covering at centre half in one game, he was fortuitously spotted by the Birmingham Juniors selectors and was offered a trial. In 1903, he turned out for the Birmingham Juniors side against Scotland Juniors and he also represented England in a junior international against the Scots. In the same year, he signed for Coventry, and made his debut in the 2-0 win over Kidderminster Harriers in January 1903. His initial stay at City, however, was brief and after only five appearances he was signed by Small Heath, who were then in the Football League.

After two years with Small Heath, Chaplin was signed by First Division Woolwich Arsenal. He remained with the Londoners for two seasons, before rejoining Coventry during the 1906/07 season. Chaplin appeared only six times during his first season back at Highfield Road. However, the following year he missed only two games, and his performances were instrumental in helping Coventry record their best ever finish of fourth in the Birmingham & District League. He was also ever present in City's cup run of the same season, which saw them reach the first round proper for the very first time, before eventually losing to Crystal Palace 4-2. Coventry were elected to the Southern League for the 1908/09 campaign, and over the next four seasons Chaplin was a regular in the side which consolidated their new-found status at this higher level. 1909/10 saw Chaplin involved in further cup success with City, as the team progressed to the quarter-finals in what became a famous run. In 1912, Chaplin's service to the club was honoured with the granting of a testimonial match. The opposition were Chelsea, who at that time played in the South Eastern Counties League, and 4,324 fans turned out to offer their thanks to a great City servant. Chaplin retired from football at the end of the 1911/12 season, signing off in his final game with a rare goal – only his eighth throughout his time at Coventry. He remained in Coventry, turning out for local side Longford FC, and working for first Courtaulds and then Humber.

	Birmingham League		FA Cup		Total	
	Apps	Goals	Apps	Goals	Apps	Goals
1902/03	5	1	0	0	5	1
1906/07	6	1	0	0	6	1
1907/08	32	4	9	0	41	4

	Southern League		FA Cup		Total	
	Apps	Goals	Apps	Goals	Apps	Goals
1908/09	35	0	3	0	38	0
1909/10	38	0	5	1	43	1
1910/11	24	0	4	0	28	0
1911/12	30	1	2	0	32	1
TOTAL	170	7	23	1	193	8

Dave Clements
Outside-left, 1964-71

Dave Clements began his career with Irish side Portadown before joining Wolves as a seventeen-year-old in January 1963. His early promise earned him a call-up to the Northern Irish youth side in the same year, and he competed for his country in the Little World Cup at Wembley. However, despite his obvious talents, he was unable to make the breakthrough into the first-team at the Molineux, and his frustration alerted the attention of a number of clubs, eager to register his services. In the summer of 1964, in the face of strong competition from Watford, Jimmy Hill managed to sign the promising youngster for a bargain fee of £1,500. It was to prove an astute piece of business, with Clements going on to offer excellent service for City over the next eight seasons.

Clements made his Coventry debut in January 1965, scoring the goal which secured City a point in the 1-1 draw with Northampton Town. In his next nine games he scored a further seven goals, and he ended the season with 9 strikes in 15 appearances. In the same year he earned his first call up to the Northern Irish side, making his international debut in the 5-0 defeat at the hands of Wales in March. It was the first of 21 caps he would win while with City, a record not surpassed until the mid 1990s. During the late 1960s, Clements was a regular in City's first team, comfortably making the transition to First Division football. He was a versatile player, who was able to play in any of the left-sided positions, but he predominantly played in his favoured role on the left-wing. Although never a regular goalscorer, Clements also possessed a fearsome left-foot shot, which netted him 29 goals for the Sky Blues.

In August 1971, the shock news was announced that Clements had been transferred to Sheffied Wednesday for a fee of £55,000. The early 1970s was a time of austerity for the Sky Blues, and Noel Cantwell was faced with the situation of having to sell before he could buy. With the purchase of Chris Chilton in mind, Clements was his chosen sacrifice necessary to raise the funds. By the time of his departure, Clements had made a total of 257 appearances for the Sky Blues over a period of seven years. At Sheffield Wednesday, Clements reverted to a left-back role, and in two years at Hillsborough, he played 78 League games for the Owls. He moved on to Everton in 1973 for £80,000, and in 1975 was appointed as manager of the Northern Irish national team. His reign was brief, and following a disastrous home international campaign in the spring of 1976, he resigned from the post. He went on to play in the NASL for New York Cosmos, ending his career playing along such greats as Pele, Beckenbauer and Chinaglia.

	League		FA Cup		League Cup		Other		Total	
	Apps	Goals	Apps	Goals	Apps	Goals	Apps	Goals	Apps	Goals
1964/65	15	9	0	0	0	0	0	0	15	9
1965/66	22 (1)	3	2	0	1	1	0	0	25 (1)	4
1966/67	40	4	1	0	3	1	0	0	44	5
1967/68	40 (1)	1	0	0	1	0	0	0	41 (1)	1
1968/69	37	3	2	0	4	1	0	0	43	4
1969/70	33	3	2	0	1	0	0	0	36	3
1970/71	40	3	1	0	5	0	4	0	50	3
1971/72	1	0	0	0	0	0	0	0	1	0
TOTAL	228 (2)	26	8	0	15	3	4	0	255 (2)	29

Mick Coop
Defender, 1966-81

Mick Coop stands third in the 'record appearances' list for City, his tally of 499 only being surpassed by Steve Ogrizovic and George Curtis. His City career spanned fifteen years and three decades from his debut against Brighton in September 1966 to his final appearance in the 1-1 draw with Nottingham Forest on the last day of the 1980/81 season.

Signed as a fifteen-year-old apprentice in 1963, Coop turned professional for City in January 1966. Primarily a right-back, Coop was adaptable in defensive positions and even turned out in the midfield on occasions. He established himself in the first team in 1968/69 and was voted the club's Player of the Year for 1969. He remained a first-team regular until 1974/75, when the emergence of Graham Oakey ousted him from the starting line-up. A loan period at York City followed between November 1974 and May 1975; however, he played only four games for the Bootham Crescent club during this time, and he returned to Highfield Road to reclaim a place in the first team, this time in a central defensive role. Coop was a regular for City throughout the late 1970s, and fulfilled the role of penalty taker, scoring 17 of his eventual total of 22 goals from the spot. A second loan spell, this time to Detroit Express in the NASL came in May 1979, before he returned to make a further 69 appearances for City during the 1979/80 and 1980/81 seasons.

His move to Derby County in July 1981 was not a successful one and, after only six months with the club, his contract was cancelled and he returned to his native Leamington. He went on to play a number of games for non-League AP Leamington during the 1982/83 season, before finally retiring in the summer of 1983. In 1985, Coop returned to Highfield Road, taking up the position of youth team coach. It was under his tutelage that Coventry recorded their first FA Youth Cup triumph in 1987. He even helped out as a player in the reserve team, appearing against Middlesborough in May 1987. Two years later, he left his position following a disagreement with manager John Sillett, and departed the world of football altogether, opting for the quieter life of an antique dealer.

	League		FA Cup		League Cup		Other		Total	
	Apps	Goals	Apps	Goals	Apps	Goals	Apps	Goals	Apps	Goals
1966/67	2 (2)	0	0	0	1	0	0	0	3 (2)	0
1967/68	13 (2)	0	0 (1)	0	1	0	0	0	14 (3)	0
1968/69	36 (1)	0	2	0	4	0	0	0	42 (1)	0
1969/70	41	0	2	0	1	0	0	0	44	0
1970/71	25	0	0	0	5	0	4	0	34	0
1971/72	13 (2)	0	1	0	1	0	4	0	19 (2)	0
1972/73	42	0	4	1	2	0	2	0	50	1
1973/74	30	5	4	1	6	1	1	0	41	7
1974/75	2 (4)	0	0	0	0	0	0	0	2 (4)	0
1975/76	42	4	3	0	2	0	0	0	47	4
1976/77	39	2	2	0	3	1	0	0	44	3
1977/78	34 (1)	6	1	0	4	0	0	0	39 (1)	6
1978/79	36	0	2	0	0	0	0	0	38	0
1979/80	31	1	2	0	1 (1)	0	0	0	34 (1)	1
1980/81	27	0	2	0	5	0	0	0	34	0
TOTAL	413 (12)	18	25 (1)	2	36 (1)	2	11	0	485 (14)	22

George Curtis
Centre-half, 1955-69; manager (with John Sillett) 1986-87

George Curtis has often been described as 'Mr Coventry City', a title which is well deserved given George's forty years of service to the Sky Blues. Having signed as a sixteen-year-old in 1955, he remained with the club until the mid-1990s; only a three-year spell on Aston Villa's books interrupted his time at Highfield Road. As a player, he made 538 appearances for City, a record only recently beaten by Steve Ogrizovic. On the managerial side, his partnership with John Sillett in the mid-1980s achieved more than any other before them in bringing a major trophy to the club for the first time. His position as one of the club's greats is unchallengeable.

Curtis was first discovered by former City player Harry Barrett, who was managing Kent side Snowdon Colliery at the time. Barrett recommended the young centre-half to City manager Jesse Carver, and in October 1955, Curtis was signed as a Coventry player. He made his debut less than a year later, in the 4-2 defeat at Newport County in April 1956 and over the next two years he gradually developed into a first-team regular. Curtis was a strong, physical centre half who earned the nickname 'Iron Man' due to his uncompromising playing style. He gained a reputation throughout the League as a fearsome competitor who gave little change to opposing forwards.

From August 1958 until September 1967, Curtis missed only a handful of games for City, and he captained the side through the rise from the Fourth Division to First. His performances earned him a number of accolades, being named City's Player of the Year in both 1960 and 1961, and also the Midlands Player of the Year in the Third Division Championship-winning season of 1963/64. He was a collossus in the City team which won the Second Division in 1967, and he looked forward to a long top-flight career with the Sky Blues; however, this was to prove not to be. Cruelly, he sustained a broken leg in only City's second game in the First Division, an injury which kept him out of the most of the rest of the inaugural campaign. He returned to the side as a regular in 1968/69, but he was never the same player after his injury, and in December 1969, after a total of 54 top-flight appearances for the Sky Blues, he transferred to Aston Villa for £25,000.

Curtis spent the final three years of his playing career at Villa Park, eventually retiring in the summer of 1972. He returned to Highfield Road in 1974, taking up a post in the commercial department. Over the next fifteen years he remained with the City backroom staff, first as commercial manager and then managing director. When Dave Mackay resigned as City manager in early 1986, Curtis was called upon to take over the reins in tandem with his former team-mate John Sillett. Thus began one of the most exciting periods of City's top-flight history.

Curtis and Sillett instilled a spirit in the side that had long been lacking, and brought out the best in players who had hitherto underperformed. Under George and John's leadership, the team played an attractive, flowing game that won the admiration of many, and began pushing into the top half of the First Division for the first time in some years. The zenith came in 1986/87, when they led City to the FA Cup final and brought home the club's first major trophy. After the Cup Final, Curtis handed over full responsibility for team affairs to Sillett and returned to a backroom position at the club. He remained on City's staff until 1994.

	League		FA Cup		League Cup			Total	
	Apps	Goals	Apps	Goals	Apps	Goals		Apps	Goals
1955/56	3	0	0	0	-	-		3	0
1956/57	19	0	0	0	-	-		19	0
1957/58	15	0	1	0	-	-		16	0
1958/59	43	0	2	0	-	-		45	0
1959/60	45	0	2	0	-	-		47	0
1960/61	46	1	3	0	2	0		51	1
1961/62	46	0	2	0	1	0		49	0
1962/63	45	0	9	1	2	0		56	1
1963/64	46	0	2	0	2	0		50	0
1964/65	41	1	1	0	4	0		46	1
1965/66	42	5	4	0	4	0		50	5
1966/67	42	2	1	0	3	0		46	2
1967/68	3 (1)	0	0	0	0	0		3 (1)	0
1968/69	28 (2)	2	2	1	3	0		33 (2)	3
1969/70	19 (1)	0	0	0	1	0		20 (1)	0
TOTAL	483 (4)	11	29	2	22	0		534 (4)	13

George Curtis during his spell as part of the management team with Greg Downs.

Gerry Daly
Midfield, 1980-84

Republic of Ireland international Gerry Daly was brought to British football by Tommy Docherty, who signed him for Manchester United in April 1973. The nineteen-year-old had shown promise while playing in his homeland for the Bohemians club, and had developed while with United into an accomplished midfielder with a cool head and a classy style. As part of the side which briefly dropped into the Second Division in 1974, Daly experienced both the highs and lows of the game, with their relegation and subsequent promotion. He also won an FA Cup losers' medal with United, and had made 143 appearances by the time of his £175,000 transfer to Derby County in 1977.

After three years at the Baseball Ground, during which time he had spent two loan spells with the New England Teamen in the NASL, Gordon Milne signed Daly for £300,000 in August 1980. Coventry, at the time, had a very youthful side, the crux of which was made up of graduates from the highly successful youth scheme. Daly was brought in to bring some much needed experience to City's midfield and to offer guidance to the youngsters. He made his debut in the 0-0 draw with Liverpool at the start of 1980/81, and established himself at the heart of City's side through the season, proving himself to be a valuable asset. He was instrumental in the League Cup run of that year, in which City reached the semi-finals for the first-time ever, before going out in a see-saw tie with West Ham.

The following season saw Dave Sexton take over from Gordon Milne as City's manager, and signalled a downturn in Daly's Highfield Road career. Daly proved to be out of favour with the new boss, and, after playing a bit part in 1981/82, was loaned out to Leicester City in January 1983. It was not until Bobby Gould succeeded Sexton that Daly once again became part of the City set-up, but his influence proved to be less significant than during his first season. He was eventually sold to Birmingham City in the summer of 1984, after just over a hundred appearances for the Sky Blues.

In the five years after leaving City, Daly moved regularly around the lower divisions, playing for Shrewsbury Town, Doncaster Rovers and Stoke City in addition to his time at St Andrews. He finally ended his League career by joining Telford United in 1989 as their player-manager.

	League		FA Cup		League Cup		Total	
	Apps	Goals	Apps	Goals	Apps	Goals	Apps	Goals
1980/81	34 (1)	8	4	2	7	1	45 (1)	11
1981/82	19	4	2	0	0	0	21	4
1982/83	2	0	0	0	0	0	2	0
1983/84	27 (1)	7	3 (1)	0	0	0	30 (2)	7
TOTAL	82 (2)	19	9 (1)	2	7	1	98 (3)	22

Jimmy Dougall
Outside right, 1919-26

Young Scottish winger Jimmy Dougall was signed for City by Harry Pollitt in December 1919. He had begun his career with Clelland Juniors, impressing with his displays on the right-wing, and he earned Scottish junior international recognition. He was briefly on the books at Motherwell, before Pollitt brought him south of the border, aged just nineteen. Over the next seven seasons, he was to provide excellent service for City, making 237 appearances as Coventry struggled to establish themselves in the Football League.

Dougall made his debut in the 2-2 draw in the FA Cup tie with Luton Town, and quickly established himself as a first-team regular. He was a skilful winger, who possessed pace and excellent crossing ability. He regularly attracted the attention of bigger clubs, and a number of offers were made by rivals eager to procure Dougall's signature. Indeed, in 1924, Manchester United offered £2,000 – a significant fee in the 1920s – for his services. All approaches were rejected by City, who were keen to hold on to one of their prized assets.

Dougall remained at Highfield Road until the summer of 1926, when he rejected the terms City were offering and left to join Reading for a fee of £555. His career at Elm Park, however, was short-lived as he broke his leg in what was only his twelfth game. The injury brought his career to a premature end and he was forced to retire at the age of only twenty-seven. After leaving the game, he returned to live in Coventry, taking up employment in the motor industry. Towards the end of the Second World War, one of Dougall's sons, also called Jimmy, turned out for Coventry. He made 22 appearances in the wartime side, but never made the team after the end of the hostilities.

	League Apps	Goals	FA Cup Apps	Goals	Total Apps	Goals
1919/20	11	1	2	0	13	1
1920/21	37	2	2	0	39	2
1921/22	32	1	2	0	34	1
1922/23	34	3	1	0	35	3
1923/24	33	3	0	0	33	3
1924/25	41	2	3	0	44	2
1925/26	38	2	1	0	39	1
TOTAL	226	14	11	0	237	14

Dion Dublin
Centre forward, 1994-98

More than a few eyebrows were raised when Phil Neal, flush with the money from Phil Babb's sale to Liverpool, announced he was spending £2 million on Dion Dublin. Dublin had been languishing in the Manchester United reserve team after his 'dream' move from Cambridge United had turned sour. A broken leg suffered shortly after his arrival at Old Trafford, meant he never had the chance to establish himself and, consequently, he had only made 6 first-team starts during his two years at United. Such limited experience at the top level warranted Dublin a significant gamble, particularly as Neal was paying twice what United had parted with for his services. It was to be a gamble that paid dividends for City, as Dublin became the highest goalscorer in City's top-flight history.

Dublin was first spotted by scouts for Norwich City whilst playing for Oakham Town. He signed as a professional for Norwich in early 1988, but he was released only a few months later. He then joined Cambridge United, initially as a non-contract trialist. Dublin's powerful presence up front was ideal for John Beck's long-ball game, and he became a regular in the side that won promotion from the Fourth to the Second Division in consecutive years. His scoring record whilst at the Abbey Stadium was 74 goals in 202 games, and it was this which alerted the attention of Alex Ferguson, and culminated in his move to Old Trafford.

Dublin's career with Coventry began with 6 goals in his first 6 games, during September and October 1994. He ended his first season as the club's leading scorer with 16 goals, a record he matched the following year, in which he was also appointed club captain. In 1996/97, his haul was down to 13, in a season marred by a seven-game ban for being sent off in two consecutive games. This disciplinary breach lead to a temporary removal of the captaincy from Dublin, but did little to mar the fans' opinion of their idol, with Dublin being voted Coventry's Player of the Year.

1997/98, however, was Dublin's finest season as a Coventry player. The campaign saw Dublin and Darren Huckerby forging an exciting and deadly partnership up front, earning England recognition for both. For Dublin, this was at full international level, and he won 3 caps, becoming the first City player to represent England since Cyrille Regis in 1987. His goalscoring reached new heights, with 23 goals in all competitions, equalling Ian Wallace's top-flight record. In the League, he netted 18, which saw him win the coveted Golden Boot award for the Premiership (jointly with Michael Owen), another first for City. Deservedly, he retained the Player of the Year award, in what proved to be his final full season with City.

Speculation regarding Dublin's future was now rife, and was fuelled by the player's apparent longing for a move. It is unfortunate that his eventual transfer to Aston Villa became decidedly bad-tempered. Villa's offer of £5 million was significantly below City's valuation for their star striker, but Dublin made it very clear he wanted to move to the Birmingham club. Protracted negotiations eventually saw the sale completed for £5.75 million, but not before Dublin had omitted himself from the squad to play a League Cup tie at Luton, bringing harsh condemnation from Gordon Strachan. It was a sorry end to a glittering Highfield Road career.

Dublin's career at Villa continued apace, until he suffered a horrific neck injury which seriously threatened to end his playing days for good. Upon his return to fitness, he has not been a regular in the Villa side and remains a squad player at Villa Park.

	League		FA Cup		League Cup			Total	
	Apps	Goals	Apps	Goals	Apps	Goals		Apps	Goals
1994/95	31	13	4	1	3	2		38	16
1995/96	34	14	3	2	1 (1)	0		38 (1)	16
1996/97	33 (1)	13	1	0	3 (1)	0		37 (1)	13
1997/98	36	18	5	4	2	1		43	23
1998/99	10	3	0	0	2	1		12	4
TOTAL	144 (1)	61	13	7	11 (2)	4		168 (3)	72

Dublin battling against Leeds in his first season for the Sky Blues.

Bob Evans
Goalkeeper, 1909-13

Bob Evans holds the distinction of being Coventry City's first ever full international, representing Wales 5 times during his stay at Highfield Road, to add to the 5 caps he had already earned, prior to joining City. Evans was an outstanding goalkeeper, his agility and skills matched by his bravery – in an era where 'keepers enjoyed very little protection.

Evans had originally played as a full-back, but was persuaded to become a 'keeper with his junior side, Stansty Villa. He joined Wrexham as an seventeen-year-old, spending five years at the Racecourse Ground, during which time he earned his first international call-up. He moved to Blackburn Rovers in 1903 for a fee of £150, and quickly became a hero at Ewood Park. In 1905, he was appointed captain of the Lancashire club, a position he held for two years. After five years with Blackburn he moved south, joining Croydon Common in the close season of 1908. He spent less than a year with Croydon, before joining Coventry in May 1909.

During his time at Coventry, Evans was recognized as one of the most able 'keepers in the country. His consistently excellent displays helped Coventry to consolidate their new-found status in the League, as well as embark on two famous cup runs. Over the course of his four years with City, Evans made 139 appearances, before injury saw him lose his first-team place towards the end of the 1912/13 season. During the summer of 1913, he left Highfield Road, joining neighbours Birmingham City for a fee of £50. By this time, he was reaching the end of his career and, after only a year with Birmingham, he moved to non-League Nuneaton Borough, where he finished his playing days.

	Southern League		FA Cup		Total	
	Apps	Goals	Apps	Goals	Apps	Goals
1909/10	34	0	6	0	40	0
1910/11	37	0	3	0	40	0
1911/12	34	0	2	0	36	0
1912/13	21	0	2	0	23	0
TOTAL	126	0	13	0	139	0

Ron Farmer
Left-half, 1958-67

It was during a Football Combination game between Birmingham City and Nottingham Forest that Billy Frith spotted the dual talents of left half, Ron Farmer, and goalkeeper, Arthur Lightening. So impressed was Frith, that he clinched the signing of the Forest duo immediately after the game, a fee of £6,000 sufficient to register the services of the pair. Thus began a decade of service to City, during which Farmer made 300 appearances and was a crucial member of the team which rose from the Fourth Division to the First in just eight years.

Farmer made his debut in November 1958 in the 5-1 thrashing of Chester City, and was ever present during the rest of the season in which City won promotion from the Fourth Division. Over the course of the campaign, he developed an excellent understanding with George Curtis and Mick Kearns, cementing the half-back line that would prove so consistent in the drive to the top flight. Farmer was a regular penalty taker, earning a reputation as a master from the spot – of the 22 penalties he took for City, he converted 21, hitting the post with his only miss. In open play, Farmer also showed himself more than able to add to City's attacking prowess, scoring with some spectacular long-range strikes, and totalling 53 goals during his City career.

After helping the team win the Second Division Championship in 1967, Farmer played only 4 games in the inaugural First Division campaign, before being superceded in the left-half role by new signing, Brian Lewis. In all, he had made 315 appearances for the Sky Blues, a total only bettered by ten players. In 1967, he was granted a free transfer in lieu of a testimonial and moved on to Notts County, in a deal which netted him £10,000. After two years at Meadow Lane, he dropped into non-League football with Grantham Town, before retiring as a player in 1970. He later returned to Highfield Road for a spell as the club's youth team coach.

	League		FA Cup		League Cup		Total	
	Apps	Goals	Apps	Goals	Apps	Goals	Apps	Goals
1958/59	26	1	0	0	-	-	26	1
1959/60	33	6	2	0	-	-	35	6
1960/61	36	3	3	2	2	0	41	5
1961/62	26	7	1	0	1	0	28	7
1962/63	22	6	5	1	1	0	28	7
1963/64	44	11	2	0	1	0	47	11
1964/65	25	3	0	0	1	0	26	3
1965/66	34 (1)	9	4	1	4	0	42 (1)	10
1966/67	32 (2)	2	1	0	2	1	35 (2)	3
1967/68	3 (1)	0	0	0	0	0	3 (1)	0
TOTAL	281 (4)	48	18	4	12	1	311 (4)	53

Mick Ferguson
Centre forward, 1971-81 and 1984

Mick Ferguson was a colossus in the City forward line of the late 1970s. He came to City as an apprentice, signing professional in December 1971. It was not until three years later that he was able to make his first team debut, in the 0-0 draw with Leeds in February 1975. Despite playing a further 11 games that season, it wasn't until 1976/77 that he became a regular. Midway through the same campaign, he linked up with Ian Wallace to form one of the most exciting strike partnerships of the modem era. During 1977/78, 'Wally' and 'Fergie' terrorised First Division defences, and despite missing the last two months of the season through injury, Ferguson scored 17 of the pair's 40 goals.

Over the next two seasons, Ferguson was plagued by injury, never appearing in more than half City's games in any season. However, when fit, his striking prowess was apparent – never more so than in November 1979, when he scored eight in four games, including four against Ipswich Town. By 1981, transfer speculation was rife, with (amongst others) Forest and Ipswich Town expressing an interest in Ferguson. It was Everton who eventually clinched his signature, when in the summer of 1981, he joined the Toffeemen for £280,000.

After a year at Goodison, Ferguson joined Birmingham City on loan, making the deal permanent in the summer of 1983. Despite starting well for the Blues, he was languishing in the reserves by the end of 1983/4, when Bobby Gould seized the opportunity to bring Ferguson back to Highfield Road as a loanee, to bolster City's battle against relegation. Three goals in seven games, including one in the crucial final game against Norwich, helped ensure City's survival, whilst consigning his own club, Birmingham City, to relegation.

	League		FA Cup		League Cup			Total	
	Apps	Goals	Apps	Goals	Apps	Goals		Apps	Goals
1974/75	12	2	0	0	0	0		12	2
1975/76	11 (4)	3	0	0	0 (2)	1		11 (6)	4
1976/77	32	13	0	0	3	2		35	15
1977/78	30	17	1	0	4	0		35	17
1978/79	16 (2)	6	0	0	1	0		17 (2)	6
1979/80	17	10	1	0	2	0		20	10
1980/81	3	0	1	0	0	0		4	0
1983/84	7	3	0	0	0	0		7	3
TOTAL	128 (6)	54	3	0	10 (2)	3		141 (8)	57

Billy Frith

Wing half, 1932-45 and 1946-47; manager 1947-48 and 1957-61

Billy Frith's links with Coventry spanned four decades and almost thirty years, with two spells as both player and manager. Signed by Harry Storer in May 1932, the young wing-half made a scoring debut in the 3-1 victory over Newport County in 1932, although he was not a regular until 1934/35. Over the next five seasons, Frith proved to he consistent and dependable attacking wing-half, and was a constant in the side which won promotion to the Second Division and pushed for the elusive place in the First.

He continued to play for City throughout the war, during which time he also 'guested' for Leicester City. He played a total of 74 wartime matches for the club and was selected for the England wartime team in 1945, although he was unable to compete due to injury. When football restarted, Frith left City to become player-manager at Port Vale. His stay at Burslem Park was short-lived, however, and he returned to City in the 1946/47 season. He played a further 8 games, taking his tally of City appearances to 177.

Towards the end of 1946/47, City manager Dick Bayliss was seriously ill and died. Frith was chosen to become Coventry manager, but only remained in the post for little over a year. With City struggling in the Second Division by November of 1948, he was sacked, his replacement being his earlier mentor, Harry Storer. Frith was very bitter about the manner in which he had been treated and left full-time football to become a teacher. By 1955, Frith's anger with City had subsided, and he returned to the club as a coach. After the upheaval of six managers in four years, Frith was finally called upon to restore some stability, and he was appointed as Harry Warren's replacement in September 1957. His first season back in the City hotseat saw Coventry fail in their attempt to finish in the top half of the Third Division (South) and drop into the newly-formed Fourth Division. To Frith's credit, he constructed a side which escaped the bottom division at the first attempt. In the following year they mounted a strong challenge for promotion to the Second, but fell short, eventually finishing fourth.

This was to be the pinnacle of Frith's career as manager, with an ageing City side going into decline as the 1960s dawned. They finished 1960/61 in a disappointing fifteenth, and made an indifferent start to the new campaign before the true disaster occurred. On 25 November, Coventry lost to non-League opponents Kings Lynn in what should have been a routine FA Cup second round tie. Frith was promptly sacked, ending his final connection with the club after twenty-nine years.

| | League | | FA Cup | | Total | |
	Apps	Goals	Apps	Goals	Apps	Goals
1932/33	3	1	0	0	3	1
1933/34	8	0	0	0	8	0
1934/35	22	0	1	0	23	0
1935/36	29	2	2	0	31	2
1936/37	29	1	3	0	32	1
1937/38	32	0	0	0	32	0
1938/39	39	0	1	0	40	0
1945/46	-	-	0	0	0	0
1946/47	7	0	1	0	8	0
TOTAL	169	4	8	0	177	4

Kevin Gallacher

Forward, 1990-93

John Sillett broke the Coventry transfer record to bring Kevin Gallacher to Highfield Road for £900,000 in January 1990. A skilful and pacy winger, he proved to be a burgeoning talent, who played exciting and creative football in his four years at City. Gallacher came from a footballing family, with his father, William, and grandfather, Patsy, both playing for Glasgow Celtic. The latest in the line of footballing Gallachers, however, started his career with Dundee United, spending seven years with the Terrors, prior to joining City. Whilst at Tannadice Park, Gallacher featured in three major finals, including the UEFA Cup final in 1987, but received only a runners-up medal in each.

Gallacher adjusted to the English game quickly, and proved an exciting attacking force for the Sky Blues. His debut came in the 3-2 win over Chelsea in early February 1990, and he was ever present for the duration of the season, netting 3 goals in his 17 games. The following year he excelled, ending the campaign as City's Player of the Year, as well as top scorer with 16 strikes. His performances earned him a recall to the Scottish side, winning the first of 10 caps whilst with the Sky Blues. Although dogged with injuries in his final two seasons with City, Gallacher continued to be inspiring on the pitch, once again finishing as top scorer in 1991/92, and creating a great deal of interest from clubs eager to register his services. Increasingly, it seemed only a matter of time before Coventry cashed in on their star player, and midway through the 1992/93 campaign, the inevitable news broke that Gallacher had been sold.

The swap deal which saw Gallacher move from City to Blackburn, with Roy Wegerle making the return journey, valued the outgoing striker at £2.5 million, making him City's most expensive export up until that time. He spent six years at Ewood Park, during which time he won a Championship medal in 1995, and further established himself as a regular Scottish international. In 1999, he moved to Newcastle United, becoming Bobby Robson's first signing for the Magpies. He played 25 times in his first season with Newcastle, but fell out of favour during 2000/01, and was released at the end of the campaign.

	League		FA Cup		League Cup		Other		Total	
	Apps	Goals	Apps	Goals	Apps	Goals	Apps	Goals	Apps	Goals
1989/90	15	3	0	0	2	0	0	0	17	3
1990/91	32	11	2	0	3	5	1	0	38	16
1991/92	33	8	1	0	4	2	1	0	39	10
1992/93	19 (1)	6	1	0	2	0	0	0	22 (1)	6
TOTAL	99 (1)	28	4	0	11	7	2	0	116 (1)	35

Ian Gibson
Midfield, 1966-70

The son of Willie Gibson, a former Hamilton centre half, Ian Gibson began his League career at the tender age of sixteen, turning out for Accrington Stanley in their 2-0 FA Cup defeat against Norwich City in 1959. Accrington's Scottish manager, Walter Galbraith, had brought his fellow countryman to the Lancashire club a year earlier, having been impressed by Gibson's performances in his 4 schoolboy internationals. After a further 8 games for Stanley in 1958/59, he moved to Bradford Park Avenue in the summer of 1959, where Galbraith had taken over as manager. Gibson was a regular throughout his three years at Park Avenue, impressing with his excellent ball control and his intricate close skill. In March 1962, Middlesborough paid the tidy sum of £40,000 to take him to Ayresome Park, where he continued to progress and was duly made captain. When Boro were relegated to the Third Division in 1966, Coventry manager, Jimmy Hill, took the opportunity to bring Gibson to Highfield Road, signing him for what was then a club record of £57,500. It was the start of four years at City, during which time Gibson became a true crowd favourite, with his dazzling midfield displays and his cultured playmaking skills. Gibson's career at City, however, got off to a rocky start. After making his debut on the opening day of the 1966/67 season, Gibson had a number of disappointing games, and came under fire from Hill, who labelled the Scot as 'undisciplined'. Gibson slapped in a transfer request, and was dropped from the side, but with City's promotion drive wavering, he was reinstated for the home game with Cardiff in November. Gibson responded with a glorious performance, netting twice as City overcame the Welshmen 3-2. Hill and Gibson managed to iron out their differences and Gibson became a crucial part of the team that won the Second Division championship in May of the following year.

Over the course of City's first two seasons in the top flight, Gibson was plagued with knee troubles which limited his appearances to just 40 in two years. However, whenever fit, his performances continued to be first-rate, making his periods of enforced absence even more frustrating. He returned to something like full fitness for the 1969/70 season, making 30 appearances in what was to be his final campaign with the club. In the close season of 1970, Noel Cantwell accepted a bid of £35,000 for Gibson from Cardiff City, bringing to an end four years as a City player, during which Gibbo had made just over 100 appearances.

Gibson remained at Ninian Park for two years, before joining Bournemouth in October 1972. He brought his League career to a close with the Cherries, dropping into non-League football, with Gateshead United in 1974.

	League		FA Cup		League Cup		Total	
	Apps	Goals	Apps	Goals	Apps	Goals	Apps	Goals
1966/67	31	8	1	0	2	0	34	8
1967/68	14 (1)	0	2	0	1	0	17 (1)	0
1968/69	17 (1)	3	0	0	4	1	21 (1)	4
1969/70	28 (1)	2	0	0	1	0	29 (1)	2
TOTAL	90 (3)	13	3	0	8	1	101 (3)	14

Terry Gibson
Centre forward, 1983-86

London-born Terry Gibson began his career with Tottenham Hotspur as an apprentice. Early promise earned him England youth honours and a debut for Spurs, just a week after his seventeenth birthday. He signed professional forms at White Hart Lane in January 1980, but was never able to command a regular first-team place and joined Coventry in the summer of 1983, after just 18 appearances for Spurs.

Gibson proved to be one of Bobby Gould's most inspired signings. He made his debut in the opening game of the 1983/84 season, scoring one of the goals in the 3-2 win over Watford. By the end of the season, he headed the goalscoring charts with 19 goals: 17 in the League campaign and 2 in the FA Cup tie with Sheffield Wednesday. Easily the highlight of his first season was the hat-trick scored against the mighty Liverpool in early December, making him the first player to achieve such a feat in over a decade.

The following year saw Coventry, once again, in a desperate struggle against relegation, and Gibson once again scoring the goals which would ensure their First Division status by the narrowest of margins – 15 League strikes, including one in the last-day victory against the Champions Elect, Everton, deservedly earned Gibson the accolade of Player of the Year.

By the start of 1985/86, interest in Gibson from other First Division clubs was growing and transfer speculation was rife. Amidst rumours that he was unsettled in the Midlands, speculation of an imminent move grew, and in January 1986, he signed for Ron Atkinson's Manchester United. The deal, which involved a swap with Alan Brazil, valued Gibson at £650,000.

The move proved an unhappy one, with Gibson making only 26 appearances for United in eighteen months. In August 1987, he left Old Trafford to link back up with Bobby Gould at Wimbledon, helping them to FA Cup success a year later. He remained with the Dons for four years, during which time he had loan spells with both Swindon and Charlton. After joining Barnet as player-coach, injury brought Gibson's playing career to an end. He is currently first team coach at Wycombe Wanderers.

	League		FA Cup		League Cup		Other		Total	
	Apps	Goals	Apps	Goals	Apps	Goals	Apps	Goals	Apps	Goals
1983/84	35 (1)	17	3	2	2	0	0	0	40 (1)	19
1984/85	38	15	2	3	2	1	0	0	42	19
1985/86	24	11	1	0	3	2	2	1	30	14
TOTAL	97 (1)	43	6	5	7	3	2	1	112 (1)	52

Gary Gillespie
Centre half, 1978-83 and 1994

Gary Gillespie was only seventeen when Gordon Milne paid £75,000 to bring him to City from Falkirk in March 1978. While with the Bairns, he had been on semi-professional terms, and had been working in a bank, as well as playing in the Scottish Second Division. Nevertheless, he had already made history by becoming the youngest captain of a first-class team whilst at Brockville Park, skippering the side when aged only sixteen. His debut for the Sky Blues came some five months later, in the opening game of the 1978/79 season at Middlesborough. Over the course of his first season, he played in 16 games and showed glimpses of the outstanding talent that was to make him one of the most accomplished defenders in the English game.

The following season, Gillespie became a regular at the heart of the City defence, forming a consistent partnership with Paul Dyson. As the 1980s dawned, Coventry possessed one of the youngest teams in the land, with Gillespie being one of the undoubted stars of the fledgling side. He missed very few games over the course of the next four seasons, establishing a reputation as both a solid and a classy centre half. His talents were recognised at international level, with 8 under-21 caps earned during his spell with the Sky Blues.

In the summer of 1983, Gillespie was one of eight City first-teamers that left Highfield Road in what became a mass exodus. Of the eight, Gillespie appeared the most reluctant to depart, but an offer of £325,000 from Liverpool was sufficient to see City part with their young centre half. By the time of his departure, Gillespie had already made over 200 first-class appearances, and was still only twenty-three. The future looked bright for one of Scotland's rising stars.

Gillespie's career at Anfield was beset with injury problems that limited his appearances for Liverpool as well as his full international career, which was restricted to only 13 caps. However, he was part of the Liverpool side that won three League Championships, as they dominated English football. Gillespie also appeared in three major finals with the Reds, ending on the losing side in the European Cup of 1985, the League Cup of 1987 and the FA Cup of 1988. Cruelly, injury forced him to miss their successful Cup finals. After eight years at Anfield, Gillespie left to join Celtic in 1991, in a deal worth £1 million. Three years later, during an injury crisis at Highfield Road, he was loaned back to the Sky Blues. His return did not quite go according to plan, with a sending-off marring his first start for the Sky Blues in eleven years. He played 3 times in his loan spell, before bidding a second, and final, farewell to Highfield Road.

	League		FA Cup		League Cup		Total	
	Apps	Goals	Apps	Goals	Apps	Goals	Apps	Goals
1978/79	14 (1)	0	0	0	1	0	15 (1)	0
1979/80	38	1	2	0	3	0	43	1
1980/81	37	1	4	0	7	0	48	1
1981/82	40	2	4	0	2	0	46	2
1982/83	42	2	3	0	3	0	48	2
1994/95	1 (1)	0	0	0	1	0	2 (1)	0
TOTAL	172 (2)	6	13	0	17	0	202 (2)	6

Bill Glazier

Goalkeeper, 1964-75

Jimmy Hill's push to strengthen his team for the Second Division saw him break the world record fee for a goalkeeper when he signed Bill Glazier from Crystal Palace in October 1964. The fee of £35,000 proved to be money well spent, as Glazier would go on to be the first choice keeper for the next decade at Highfield Road, completing 402 appearances in all competitions for City.

Born in Nottingham in 1943, Glazier's introduction to the footballing world came at Torquay United where he combined his job on the ground staff with playing for the reserves in the Western League. He then moved on to Palace where he spent three seasons as the first-choice keeper, clocking up 106 appearances. His City debut came at Fratton Park for the 2-0 win over Portsmouth, and his performances over the course of his debut season earned him three appearances for the England under-23 team. He was strongly tipped for full international honours – however, a broken leg in April 1965 effectively brought his international career to an end. The injury kept him out of first-team action for a full year, his return coming seven games before the conclusion of the 1965/66 season.

Glazier was a crucial part of the Second Division championship-winning side of 1966/7, missing only one game during the season. Over the following seven seasons, his performances would prove to be a major factor in preventing City return to the Second. His consistency in the City nets was rewarded in 1970 with an appearance for the Football League side against the Scottish League. Glazier remained City's first choice custodian until the end of the 1973/74 season, when Neil Ramsbottom superceded him. In 1974/75 he made only eight appearances. However, in November 1974, his years of service to City were rewarded with a testimonial match against the England World Cup winning team of 1966. 15,525 turned out to witness an entertaining 6-6 draw in a fitting tribute to the ten years of service Glazier had given the Sky Blues.

In July 1975, Glazier was transferred to Brentford for a fee of £12,500. He made only nine appearances at Griffin Park, before injury forced his retirement from the game.

| | League | | FA Cup | | League Cup | | Other | | Total | |
	Apps	Goals	Apps	Goals	Apps	Goals	Apps	Goals	Apps	Goals
1964/65	24	0	1	0	0	0	0	0	25	0
1965/66	7	0	0	0	0	0	0	0	7	0
1966/67	41	0	1	0	3	0	0	0	45	0
1967/68	40	0	2	0	1	0	0	0	43	0
1968/69	42	0	2	0	5	0	0	0	49	0
1969/70	40	0	2	0	1	0	0	0	43	0
1970/71	40	0	1	0	5	0	3	0	49	0
1971/72	37	0	2	0	1	0	4	0	44	0
1972/73	28	0	4	0	2	0	2	0	36	0
1973/74	40	0	6	0	6	0	1	0	53	0
1974/75	7	0	0	0	1	0	0	0	8	0
TOTAL	346	0	21	0	25	0	10	0	402	0

Bobby Gould

Centre forward, 1963-68; manager 1983-84 and 1992-93

Bobby Gould belongs to a very select group of players who were both born in Coventry and went on to have successful careers at Highfield Road. Gould made his first team debut in October 1963 at the age of seventeen, although over the next two years his opportunities for first team football were very much curtailed by the consistency of centre forward George Hudson.

It was not until Hudson departed for Northampton Town in early 1966, that Gould was able to establish himself as a first-team regular. During the promotion season of 1966/67, he scored 24 League goals ranking him as the Second Division's top scorer. Highlights of the season included a hat-trick in the 5-0 drubbing of Ipswich Town and a run of six consecutive scoring matches in late March and early April. Injuries hampered Gould's opportunities in City's inaugural First Division campaign, his appearances limited to 14 (and one as substitute). Despite this, he still managed to score 8 times, including a memorable brace in the battling 3-3 draw against Nottingham Forest, and Coventry's first ever top-flight hat-trick in the 5-1 victory over Burnley.

In February 1968 he transferred to Arsenal for £90,000. In his two years with the Gunners he scored 42 goals in 89 appearances. Once he left Highbury for Wolves in 1970, Gould was never able to settle for more than eighteen months at any of his future clubs. Following spells with West Brom, both Bristol clubs, West Ham and a second period at Wolves, he finally ended his playing career at Hereford United, hanging up his boots in 1980. In 1983, he returned to Highfield Road for his first spell as manager. It was a time of turmoil for City, with many players disenchanted following the sacking of Dave Sexton. During the close season of 1983, no fewer than eight first-team regulars left the club and Gould was faced with the onerous task of building up a team from the skeleton squad that remained. There followed a frantic period of activity in the transfer market, with Gould enlisting the services of twenty-five players in just eighteen months. His knowledge of the lower divisions enabled him to make a number of very shrewd signings, including seven of those who would go on to the Cup-winning side of 1987. However, he was unable to craft his new recruits into a successful side and, with City continuing to struggle, he was sacked in December 1984.

Following periods in charge of Bristol Rovers, West Brom and, famously, the FA Cup-winning Wimbledon, he returned to Highfield Road for a second spell as manager in 1992. Again he was to remain for less than eighteen months, resigning in October of the following year after City's 5-1 defeat at the hands of Queens Park Rangers. In his one full season back in charge, Coventry finished fifteenth in the newly-formed Premier League.

	League		FA Cup		League Cup			Total	
	Apps	Goals	Apps	Goals	Apps	Goals		Apps	Goals
1963/64	2	0	0	0	0	0		2	0
1964/65	8	3	0	0	1	1		9	4
1965/66	17 (2)	5	1	0	0	0		18 (2)	5
1966/67	38 (1)	24	1	0	3	1		42 (1)	25
1967/68	13 (1)	8	0	0	1	0		14 (1)	8
TOTAL	78 (4)	40	2	0	5	2		85 (4)	42

Micky Gynn
Midfield, 1983-93

Micky Gynn, or Michael, as he preferred to be known, came to Coventry in the transfer whirlwind that was the summer of 1983. As with most of Bobby Gould's signings, he had been plying his trade in the lower divisions, in his case with his hometown side of Peterborough United. He had been at London Road for four years, after signing as a professional in April 1979, and had gained a reputation as an attacking midfielder with a keen eye for goal. An offer of £60,000 was sufficient to acquire Gynn's services and start a career at Highfield Road which would last ten years and almost 300 games. At 5ft 3in, he was one of the shortest players in City's history; nevertheless, he was a battling performer who was tireless in the centre of the park. Ever popular with the crowd, he was a skilful and attack-minded player, who was a constant handful for opponents.

Gynn made his debut on the opening day of the 1983/84 season, but was unfortunate enough to sustain an injury in his first game, keeping him out of action for two months. He went on to make 28 appearances in his first campaign, scoring 2 goals. Over the course of the next few years, Gynn established himself as a valuable squad member for the Sky Blues, but it was in the Cup triumph of 1987 that Gynn truly came to prominence and earned a lasting place in the annals of Sky Blue history. He was tireless in each of the FA Cup games he played, scoring vital goals – which defeated Stoke City in the fourth round and pulled City back on terms against Leeds in the semi-final. As a result of Brian Borrows' untimely injury, Gynn was able to start the final, and had an excellent game as the Sky Blues won their first major trophy.

Gynn continued to be a squad player for two seasons after the FA Cup success, before holding down a regular first-team place in 1989/90 and 1990/91. However, during his last two seasons, Gynn was dogged by injury problems, which limited his appearances. He finally left Highfield Road on a free transfer in August 1993, in order to join First Division Stoke City.

	League Apps	League Goals	FA Cup Apps	FA Cup Goals	League Cup Apps	League Cup Goals	Other Apps	Other Goals	Total Apps	Total Goals
1983/84	20 (3)	2	2 (1)	0	2	0	0	0	24 (4)	2
1984/85	32 (7)	4	2	0	2	0	0	0	36 (7)	4
1985/86	6 (6)	1	0	0	1 (1)	0	1	0	8 (7)	1
1986/87	16 (6)	5	3 (1)	2	0 (3)	0	1	0	20(10)	7
1987/88	19 (6)	3	2	0	3	2	3	1	27 (6)	6
1988/89	8	1	0	0	2	3	0	0	10	4
1989/90	31 (3)	3	1	0	6	1	1	1	39 (3)	5
1990/91	35	8	4	2	5	1	0	0	44	11
1991/92	21 (2)	3	1	0	1	0	0	0	23 (2)	3
1992/93	18 (2)	2	0 (1)	0	0	0	0	0	18 (3)	2
TOTAL	206(35)	32	15 (3)	4	22 (4)	7	6	2	249(42)	45

Mark Hateley
Centre forward, 1978-83

Mark Hateley arguably proved to be the most successful graduate of City's fertile youth policy of the late 1970s. Unfortunately, as has become the pattern with Coventry, the glory days would not come until after he left Highfield Road, and, sadly, Hateley proved all too keen to depart in search of success elsewhere once he had established himself with the club. The acrimonious nature of his departure in the close season of 1983 left a bitter taste with many City supporters and took the shine off the otherwise welcome sight of a home-grown talent come good.

Although he made his debut in May 1979, it was not until 1980/81 that Hateley began to establish himself in the first-team at Highfield Road. The intervening period saw sporadic appearances: 5 in 1979/80 as well as a spell on loan with American side Detroit Express. After featuring in the League Cup run of 1981, during which Hateley scored twice, he earned a regular place in the starting line-up during 1981/82, top-scoring for the club with 18 goals. He continued his rich vein of form the following year, scoring 11 in what was to be his final season with Coventry. In the close season of 1983, Hateley was out of contract and made no bones about his desire to leave City. Portsmouth made a meagre offer of £50,000, increased to £190,000 at a tribunal, and Hately was on his way to Fratton Park. In all he had made 111 appearances for the Sky Blues, scoring 34 goals.

Hateley remained at Fratton Park for a single but eventful season. He scored 25 times for Pompey, and significantly made the step up from the England under-21 team to the full squad. Hateley's performances on England's South American tour in June 1984, including his goal against the Brazilians in the Maracana, alerted the attention of Europe's biggest clubs, and in the summer of 1984 Hateley joined AC Milan for £1 million. After three seasons in Serie A, he linked up with Glen Hoddle at Monaco, remaining in France until 1990, when he returned to Britain to join Rangers.

Rangers dominated Scottish football during Hateley's spell at Ibrox, his prolific partnership with Ally McCoist contributing to five League Championship successes and two Scottish FA Cups. After an absence of eleven years, he returned to the English game with QPR in 1995, and also had a period on loan with Leeds, before a second and final spell at Ibrox. In the summer of 1997, Hateley moved into management, embarking on an eventful but ultimately unsuccessful period as player-manager with Hull City. He was sacked by Hull in November 1998 and, in the summer of 1999, joined Ross County.

	League		FA Cup		League Cup		Total	
	Apps	Goals	Apps	Goals	Apps	Goals	Apps	Goals
1978/79	1	0	0	0	0	0	1	0
1979/80	2(2)	0	1	0	0	0	3(2)	0
1980/81	17(2)	3	2(1)	0	6	2	25(3)	5
1981/82	31(2)	13	4	4	2	1	37(2)	18
1982/83	35	9	3	2	0	0	38	11
TOTAL	86(6)	25	10(1)	6	8	3	104(7)	34

Frank Herbert

Inside/outside left, 1922-29

Frank 'Cute' Herbert made a name for himself in local football. He became a local hero whilst playing for Foxford United in the Coventry and Warwickshire League, achieving the amazing feat of scoring over 100 goals in a single season. He stayed at Foxford for three seasons, before joining Bedworth United and then Exhall Colliery, combining his football with work down the mine. It was whilst playing for Exhall that Herbert was spotted by Coventry manager Albert Evans, who wasted no time in signing him for City. Indeed the story goes that Evans waited for Herbert at the pit head in order to sign him up for the club, so impressed was he with the striker's performance in the Birmingham Junior Cup semi-final for Exhall at the Butts Stadium.

Herbert was an instantly recognisable figure, with his close-cropped slicked back hair and his bustling style of play. He made his City debut as a centre-forward against Stockport on 18 November 1922. However his favoured and most effective position was on the left flank, and it was as inside or outside left that he made the majority of his appearances for Coventry. During 1922/23 he made a further ten appearances, registering two goals.

Over the next two seasons, Herbert established himself as a first-team regular, in a City side struggling in the Second Division. He top scored in 1923/24 with 12 goals, but only managed 7 the following year as City finished bottom of the division and were relegated. In the lower division Herbert flourished and began scoring with regularity. In 1925/26, Coventry's only ever season in the Third Division (North), he notched 22 goals, including a memorable hat-trick in the 7-1 drubbing of Rotherham United in November. The following year, when City competed in the Third Division (South), he top-scored again with 26 goals, 24 of which came in the league. His haul in 1926/27 included a New Year 'special' when Herbert scored four in the 5-1 victory over Watford on 1 January 1927.

Herbert continued on City's left flank for a further two years, scoring regularly but never as prolifically as between 1925 and 1927. He was plagued by niggling injuries during his final two years at City which limited his appearances and hastened his decision to move on into the non-league game. By the time he left City to join non-league Brierley Hill Alliance in 1929, he had amassed a total of 87 goals for City, which was a record at the time (although was soon superceded by the great Clarrie Bourton). He remained in the area after leaving City, and became a local publican at the Beehive Inn in Bedworth.

	League		FA Cup		Total	
	Apps	Goals	Apps	Goals	Apps	Goals
1922/23	11	2	0	0	11	2
1923/24	34	12	2	0	36	12
1924/25	31	5	3	2	34	7
1925/26	38	22	1	0	39	22
1926/27	38	24	3	2	41	26
1927/28	31	14	2	0	33	14
1928/29	5	4	1	0	6	4
TOTAL	188	83	12	4	200	87

1923/24 Coventry team. From left to right, Back row: Finlay, Allon, Jones, Best, Foster, Richmond, H. Lake (assistant trainer), Dougall. Middle row: Randel, MacLachlan, Shea, Winship, Herbert, Wood. Front row: Storey, Rowley.

Brian Hill
Midfield, 1958-71

When Brian Hill made his debut for Coventry City, he became the youngest player ever to play in a first-class game for the Sky Blues, at just 16 years and 273 days. Although that record has since been surpassed, with Gary McSheffrey beating him by 75 days, he remains the youngest ever goalscorer for his strike in that first game. It marked the start of thirteen years' service for the Sky Blues, during which time he progressed with the club from Third Division to First, via the Fourth. Indeed, Hill actually played in five divisions for City, making his debut in the final season of the Third Division (South). He was a valuable player, whose versatility offered the side an extra dimension, being able to play effectively in any of the defensive or midfield positions. In his time at Highfield Road, he achieved the feat of playing in every outfield numbered shirt, a testimony to his adaptability.

Hill made his debut against Gillingham in April 1958, however, it was not until 1962/63 that he became a first-team regular. He blossomed under his namesake, Jimmy, establishing himself in Hill's first season as manager. Between 1962 and 1964, he played predominantly at wing-half, gaining a reputation as an excellent man-marker. By 1965, his name was being mentioned as a possible England player, though an international call-up never came. During the late 1960s, Hill was plagued by niggling injuries which restricted his appearances. He found no difficulty in making the transition up the divisions and played, whenever fit, up until 1969. As the 1970s dawned, however, Hill's outings became more infrequent, and he played his final game for the Sky Blues on Boxing Day 1970. In all, he made 284 appearances for City.

In October 1971, Hill moved on to Torquay United, but was unable to settle on the South Coast, and soon returned to see out his playing days with Bedworth United.

	League		FA Cup		League Cup		Other			Total	
	Apps	Goals	Apps	Goals	Apps	Goals	Apps	Goals		Apps	Goals
1957/58	1	1	0	0	-	-	0	0		1	1
1958/59	10	0	0	0	-	-	0	0		10	0
1959/60	8	1	1	0	-	-	0	0		9	1
1960/61	10	1	0	0	1	0	0	0		11	1
1961/62	9	0	2	0	1	0	0	0		12	0
1962/63	37	1	9	0	1	0	0	0		47	1
1963/64	40	2	2	0	1	1	0	0		43	3
1964/65	28	0	1	0	1	0	0	0		30	0
1965/66	22	0	3	0	4	0	0	0		29	0
1966/67	15 (1)	0	0	0	1	0	0	0		16 (1)	0
1967/68	16 (2)	1	2 (1)	0	0	0	0	0		18 (3)	1
1968/69	31	0	2	0	5	0	0	0		38	0
1969/70	8 (1)	0	0	0	0	0	0	0		8 (1)	0
1970/71	5	0	0	0	1	0	1	0		7	0
TOTAL	240 (4)	7	22 (1)	0	16	1	1	0		279 (5)	8

Peter Hill
Forward, 1948-62

Peter Hill ranks alongside names such as George Curtis and George Mason as one of the club's most loyal servants. As a player, he served Coventry, his only professional club, for fourteen years from August 1948 until his retirement in 1962. Further spells as both trainer and kit manager extended his connections with City to over forty years.

Born in Heanor, Derbyshire on 8 August 1931, Hill began his playing days as a junior with Rutland United, before joining City's nursery side Modern Machines in 1946. He signed for Coventry two years later and made his debut in the 2-1 defeat against Sheffield Wednesday at Hillsborough in February 1949. He made only a handful of appearances during his first four seasons, and it was not until 1952/53 that he earned a regular place in the first-team. Operating at inside-left, he made 36 appearances during the course of 1952/53, scoring 13 goals, his best season tally during his time with City. A particular highlight was his first hat-trick in the 3-0 victory over Leyton Orient in September 1952.

After a disappointing campaign in 1953/54, during which Hill made only 17 appearances and failed to score, he switched to inside-right in time for the 1954/55 season, scoring 8 times in 39 matches. He varied between inside right and inside left for the next three years before moving to the right wing in 1958/59, a position he occupied for the remainder of his career. He continued with City for three seasons following their promotion from the Fourth and retired in 1962 after 303 appearances. At the time of his retirement, Hill was still only thirty years old and one wonders how high in the all-time appearance charts he could stand today, had he continued playing into his thirties.

Hill's achievements in front of goal are worthy of particular mention. Whilst never a prolific goalscorer, Hill's longevity in the side allowed him to amass a total of 77 strikes for Coventry, a total only bettered by five other players.

After his retirement, Hill took up the position of club trainer, remaining at Highfield Road in this capacity for a further five years. He returned to City once more in 1988 as kit man. Few have served City better over such a long period as Peter Hill. His commitment and loyalty to Coventry City makes him an unsung hero.

	League		FA Cup		League Cup		Total	
	Apps	Goals	Apps	Goals	Apps	Goals	Apps	Goals
1948/49	3	0	0	0	-	-	3	0
1949/50	5	2	0	0	-	-	5	2
1950/51	1	0	0	0	-	-	1	0
1951/52	5	0	1	0	-	-	6	0
1952/53	34	12	2	1	-	-	36	13
1953/54	17	0	0	0	-	-	17	0
1954/55	35	8	4	0	-	-	39	8

1955/56	31	6	0	0	-	-	31	6
1956/57	24	10	1	0	-	-	25	10
1957/58	38	10	2	1	-	-	40	11
1958/59	25	6	2	2	-	-	27	8
1959/60	25	6	2	0	-	-	27	6
1960/61	33	12	3	0	0	0	36	12
1961/62	9	1	1	0	0	0	10	1
TOTAL	285	73	18	4	0	0	303	77

Peter Hill with team-mates Brian Nicholas (left) and Lol Harvey (right).

Bert Holmes
Outside left, 1911-14 and 1914-15

Born in Mansfield, Bert Holmes began his playing career in his hometown with Mansfield Mechanics, before signing for Coventry in the close season of 1911. Holmes was a talented winger, who combined pace and strength with excellent crossing ability. His presence on the left flank offered a balance to the City side, ably supplied by Harry Parkes from the right – a wing pairing that served City with excellence, up until the outbreak of the First World War.

Holmes made his debut on the opening day of the 1911/12 season, in the 2-1 defeat at the hands of Northampton Town. Over the course of the season, he established himself as a first-team regular, making 32 appearances and scoring 3 goals, as Coventry finished sixth in the First Division of the Southern League.

He was ever present the following year, scoring 8 goals (including a memorable hat-trick in the epic 4-4 draw with Northampton). A suspension for 'training irregularities' interrupted his run in the side during the following campaign, in which he played 27 times and scored 6 goals. Holmes left City, briefly, in early 1914, to join Hearts. After only a month and 3 games in Scotland, he returned to Highfield Road, where he remained up until the end of the 1914/15 season. With the war underway, Holmes brought an end to his career at Highfield Road in the summer of 1915, joining Portsmouth, after four years and 108 appearances on City's left flank.

| | Southern League | | FA Cup | | Total | |
	Apps	Goals	Apps	Goals	Apps	Goals
1911/12	30	3	2	0	32	3
1912/13	38	8	2	0	40	8
1913/14	26	6	1	0	27	6
1914/15	8	0	1	0	9	0
TOTAL	102	17	6	0	108	17

Jim Holton
Centre half, 1977-81

Jim Holton was a big and powerfully-built defender, framed in the mould of the traditional British centre half. A fiercesome competitor, Holton was an uncompromising tackler, who proved himself to be the worthy adversary of any forward. He began his career with Celtic, but moved south to join West Brom in 1968, whilst still only seventeen. He played in the Baggies' Youth Cup-winning side of 1969, and spent three years at the Hawthorns, before moving to Shrewsbury in 1971. After two years at Gay Meadow, Tommy Docherty brought him to Old Trafford for a fee of £80,000, and it was at United that Holton came to prominence in the English game. He established himself quickly in the United first team, proving to be a real favourite of the fans with his battling performances. It was whilst at United that Holton was selected for the Scottish national side, featuring in the squad that travelled to the 1974 World Cup finals in Germany. Holton's career at Old Trafford was effectively ended by a broken leg, sustained in December 1975. After regaining his fitness, he was languishing in the reserve side when he suffered the misfortune of breaking his leg a second time and, once recovered, United allowed him to move on. He joined Sunderland in September 1976, but after only six months in the North-East, was brought to City by Gordon Milne for a fee of £50,000. He was to prove a shrewd acquisition, giving City excellent service through the late 1970s.

Holton arrived at Highfield Road in the midst of a tense relegation battle at the end of the 1976/77 season. He was thrust into the first team immediately, adding extra strength to the defence and helping City to a last-ditch survival in the famous draw with Bristol City on the last day of the season. Over the next three years, Holton was a regular in the heart of the City defence and became a real favourite with the Highfield Road crowd. He was a fiercely committed player, who never gave less than his best for the Sky Blues, an ethos that was much-valued by the fans. He eventually lost his first-team place in January 1980, being superceded by the emerging Paul Dyson, and spent two years playing in the reserves, before his transfer to Sheffield Wednesday in the close season of 1981. He finished his League career at Hillsborough and retired to become a publican in Coventry before his premature death in 1993.

	League		FA Cup		League Cup		Total	
	Apps	Goals	Apps	Goals	Apps	Goals	Apps	Goals
1976/77	8	0	0	0	0	0	8	0
1977/78	25	0	0	0	3	1	28	1
1978/79	34	0	2	0	1	0	37	0
1979/80	24	0	0	0	3	0	27	0
TOTAL	91	0	2	0	7	1	100	1

Keith Houchen

Centre forward, 1986-89

Keith Houchen was a lower division journeyman when John Sillett signed him for the Sky Blues in June 1986. After beginning his career as an apprentice with Chesterfield, he spent time with Hartlepool, Orient, Scunthorpe and York, before joining Coventry in a deal worth £50,000. Although never a regular for the Sky Blues, Houchen's place among the club's greats was assured in the glorious cup run of 1987. He had already made a name for himself in the Cup while at York, scoring the winning goal in their famous victory over Arsenal in 1985. He continued his love affair with the competition at Highfield Road, earning a 'Roy of the Rovers' reputation, and he was viewed as a lucky charm by many fans. It began at Old Trafford in the fourth round, when Houchen managed to scramble the goal that dispatched the Reds out of the competition. Then, in the quarter-final against Sheffield Wednesday, Houchen netted twice as City won 3-1.

The semi-final saw a return to Hillsborough for City and the classic encounter with Leeds United. With the score at 1-1, Houchen struck, pouncing on a rebound from a Leeds defender before side-stepping Mervyn Day and slotting the ball home. Leeds eventually equalised and it took an extra-time winner from Bennett to secure City's first trip to Wembley. It is undoubtedly Houchen's strike on the big day itself which will forever be remembered by City fans. With Spurs leading 2-1, Houchen spectacularly dived full-length to meet a Dave Bennett cross and head past Clemence. It was a stunning goal and widely reckoned to be one of the finest in recent FA Cup Final history.

With the start of the new season, Houchen returned from the glories of the Cup, to being a squad player at Highfield Road, always second to David Speedie in the battle for the front spot. Over the next two seasons he played forty more games before transferring to Hibernian for £300,000 in March 1989. His stay in Edinburgh lasted two years joining Port Vale in 1991 He returned to Hartlepool two years later where he spent his final season as player/manager.

	League		FA Cup		League Cup		Other		Total	
	Apps	Goals	Apps	Goals	Apps	Goals	Apps	Goals	Apps	Goals
1986/87	20	2	5	5	0	0	0 (1)	0	25 (1)	7
1987/88	13 (8)	3	0	0	2	0	1	0	16 (8)	3
1988/89	10 (3)	2	0 (1)	0	0 (1)	0	1	0	11 (5)	2
TOTAL	43 (11)	7	5 (1)	5	2 (1)	0	2 (1)	0	52 (14)	12

Darren Huckerby
Forward, 1996-99

Darren Huckerby was the type of player who could delight and frustrate – often in equal proportions. On his day he was one of the finest young talents in the country, possessing devastating pace, intricate close skill and a fine eye for goal. He shone in the City front line, linking up with Dion Dublin to produce one of the most effective strike forces in the 1997/98 season. At the end of that campaign he rightfully earned a nomination for the PFA Young Player of the Year award, and seemed destined for great things. However, he was all too prone to lapses in form, during which times his runs more often lead to dead ends, and his attacking forays with either wasted chances or offside positions. Ultimately it was this inconsistency which led to his departure from Coventry in 1999, and his subsequent disappointment at Leeds United. He is still remembered with great fondness at Highfield Road, however, and the memory of his last-minute winner against Manchester United in December 1997, will last in the minds of Sky Blue fans for many years to come.

Nottingham-born Huckerby began his career with Lincoln City before signing for Newcastle for £400,000 in November 1995. His year in the North-East proved frustrating, with Huckerby making only two substitute appearances for the Magpies before being loaned out for a period with Millwall, and then being allowed to join City for £1 million in November of 1996. He made his debut in the same month, coming on as a substitute in the 2-1 defeat against Aston Villa and, from December, was a regular throughout the remainder of the season, scoring 7 goals in 29 games.

During the 1997/98 season, Huckerby was a revelation and his strike-partnership with Dublin one of the most talked about in the Premiership. He was at the top of his game throughout the campaign, and netted 15 times, including the spectacular strike against Manchester United. His performances earned him international recognition at both under-21 and 'B' levels, with the more hopeful of City fans speculating on a call-up to the full side in time for the World Cup. His fine form continued into the following season, the highlight coming with consecutive hat-tricks in the games against Macclesfield and Nottingham Forest. He ended the season with 12 goals, to bring his tally for City to 34.

The 1999/2000 season was only two games old when the shock announcement was made that Huckerby had been sold to Leeds United for £5.5 million. The logic of this move was confirmed shortly afterwards with the funds raised financing the purchase of Robbie Keane from Wolves. Huckerby's time at Elland Road was a disappointment and, unable to hold down a regular first-team spot, he was transferred to Manchester City in December 2000.

	League		FA Cup		League Cup		Total	
	Apps	Goals	Apps	Goals	Apps	Goals	Apps	Goals
1996/97	21 (4)	5	4	2	0	0	25 (4)	7
1997/98	32 (2)	14	5	1	0(1)	0	37 (3)	15
1998/99	30(3)	9	3	3	2	0	35 (3)	12
1999/2000	1	0	0	0	0	0	1	0
TOTAL	84 (9)	28	12	6	2(1)	0	98(10)	34

George Hudson
Centre forward, 1963-66

George Hudson faced a difficult reception at Highfield Road, following his arrival from Peterborough in April 1963. He had been brought to the club as a replacement for crowd favourite, Terry Bly, who had been a scoring sensation during the early part of the season. Bly had netted 29 goals in his first 41 games for the club, and many questioned Jimmy Hill's judgement when he was dropped in favour of Hudson. It was to be a gamble that paid off for City. Hudson would go on to be a prolific scorer for the Sky Blues during his three years with the club, whilst the goals dried up for Bly, and within eighteen months, he had dropped into non-League football with Grantham Town.

Born in Manchester on 14 March 1937, Hudson signed for his first League club, Blackburn Rovers, in December 1957. After three years at Ewood Park, he transferred to fellow Lancashire club, Accrington Stanley, for whom he scored 35 goals in only 44 League games. From Accrington he moved to Peterborough in October 1961, and continued scoring regularly, up until his transfer to Coventry eighteen months later.

Hudson was top scorer for Coventry in each of the three seasons he started with the club. His best haul came the Third Division championship-winning season of 1963/64, when he netted 28 goals in all competitions. By the time of his departure from the club in March 1966, Hudson had scored 75 in just 129 games.

The nature of Hudson's departure, again, caused much consternation with City fans. As with the sale of Bly, many questioned Hill's judgement in parting with Hudson when he was still the team's most potent striker. However, it again appeared that Hill's judgement had been shrewd, with Hudson never finding the same scoring touch once he had left Highfield Road. Within a year of his move to Northampton, he was transferred to Tranmere Rovers, where he saw out his first-class career. After leaving the game, he went to work for the *Mirror* at their Manchester presses.

	League		FA Cup		League Cup			Total	
	Apps	Goals	Apps	Goals	Apps	Goals		Apps	Goals
1962/63	15	6	0	0	0	0		15	6
1963/64	32	24	2	3	2	1		36	28
1964/65	38	19	1	0	4	5		43	24
1965/66	28	13	3	2	4	2		35	17
TOTAL	113	62	6	5	10	8		129	75

George Hudson.

Willie Humphries
Outside right, 1962-65

It took a great deal of persuasion for Jimmy Hill to tempt Willie Humphries back into English football with Coventry in 1962. In 1958, Belfast-born Humphries had signed for Leeds, and had suffered a disastrous season at Elland Road, before returning to Ireland. Despite his reluctance to try his hand in the English League for a second time, Hill managed to coax the right-winger to Highfield Road, and made him his first signing as manager in April 1962. The move was an instant success, with Humphries establishing himself as a fixture on City's right flank. His delightful skill and excellent crossing from the wing terrorized opponents, and made him an excellent asset in City's rise to the Second Division. He also resurrected his international career at Highfield Road, being selected for the Northern Irish side while still a Third Division player.

Humphries had began his playing career with Irish club, Ards, before his ill-fated move to Elland Road in 1958. He had returned to the Irish side in 1959, and while on their books had earned a 'B' international cap, and had also represented the Irish League side on 8 occasions. In his first full season with City, Humphries became an instant success. Missing only 6 games in the entire campaign, he became a firm favourite with the fans with his attacking forays. As well as creating many chances, Humphries wasn't goal-shy himself, weighing in with 10 in his first campaign. 1962 also saw Humphries gain his first call-up to the full Northern Irish side, his debut coming in the 4-0 defeat at the hands of the Netherlands. It would be the first of 10 caps he won whilst a City player.

In the championship season of 1963/64, Humphries played in all but 6 games, scoring 11 goals. He made the transition to Second Division football smoothly, however, with the emergence of Dave Clements on the left side, Jimmy Hill had an abundance of high quality wing players, and was able move Ronnie Rees to his favoured position on the right. Consequently, Humphries was surplus to requirements, and sold on to Swansea Town for a fee of £14,000 in March 1965. In his spell at City, he had made 126 appearances, scoring 24 goals. After three years at the Vetch, in which time Humphries earned a further 4 international caps, he moved back to Ireland, rejoining Ards and later becoming their manager.

	League Apps	League Goals	FA Cup Apps	FA Cup Goals	League Cup Apps	League Cup Goals	Total Apps	Total Goals
1961/62	1	0	0	0	0	0	1	0
1962/63	41	10	9	0	1	0	51	10
1963/64	40	10	2	0	2	1	44	11
1964/65	27	3	1	0	2	0	30	3
TOTAL	109	23	12	0	5	1	126	24

Ernie Hunt

Forward, 1968-73

Ernie Hunt will always be remembered by the Sky Blue faithful as one of Coventry's greatest 'entertainers' of the modern era, combining style and flair in his football – together with an irreverant sense of humour which he often brought with him to the pitch.

Hunt began his playing career for his hometown club of Swindon, where he took the field alongside such greats as Mike Summerbee and Bobby Woodruff. He played over 200 games for the Wiltshire club, notching 82 goals before joining Wolves for £40,000 in September of 1965. It was during his time at the Molineux that he represented England at under-23 level, turning out three times in international colours. From Wolves, Hunt moved on to Everton, but, finding himself on the fringes of the team, he accepted Noel Cantwell's offer to join the Sky Blues, and in March 1968 signed up at Highfield Road for a sum of £68,000.

Hunt arrived at City in the midst of a relegation battle as they struggled to survive in their first season in the top flight. He made seven appearances in the side which escaped the drop with a point at the Dell on the last day of the season, and consolidated his place in the City forward line the following year, missing only three games in 1968/69. Hunt scored 13 during his first full season, a figure he matched in both 1970/71 and 1971/72. In all, he scored 51 goals for the Sky Blues, but none will be remembered more than the famous donkey-kick goal against Everton in October 1970. He remained a first-team regular until 1972, but injury problems and the arrival of Colin Stein signalled a downturn in his City career. He played only a handful of games during his final two seasons at Highfield Road, and was loaned out to Doncaster Rovers in January 1973. He finally left in December of the same year, joining Bristol City. After two years at Ashton Gate he moved into the non-League game with a spell at Atherstone United to bring his playing career to a close.

In an unfortunate postscript to Hunt's links with City, he briefly hit the headlines in the late 1980s with allegations of match-fixing at City in the early 1970s. Nothing came of his 'revelations', which were sold to a Sunday tabloid, and the net result was nothing more than a tarnishing of Hunt's reputation among City fans of the time.

	League		FA Cup		League Cup		Other		Total	
	Apps	Goals	Apps	Goals	Apps	Goals	Apps	Goals	Apps	Goals
1967/68	6 (1)	1	0	0	0	0	0	0	6 (1)	1
1968/69	39	11	2	0	5	2	0	0	46	13
1969/70	30 (1)	9	2	0	1	0	0	0	33 (1)	9
1970/71	29 (2)	10	1	1	4	1	4	1	38 (2)	13
1971/72	26 (1)	12	1 (1)	0	1	0	4	1	32 (2)	13
1972/73	7	2	0	0	0	0	0	0	7	2
1973/74	3 (1)	0	0	0	0	0	1	0	4 (1)	0
TOTAL	140 (6)	45	6 (1)	1	11	3	9	2	166 (7)	51

Steve Hunt
Midfield, 1978-84

Few players can lay claim to have played with such greats as Franz Beckenbauer and Pele during their career, but Steve Hunt had the enviable honour of playing alongside both in the star-studded line-up of the New York Cosmos team in the late 1970s. He spent a year in the NASL, after three years at Villa Park during which he had made little impact on the first team. Whilst in America, he helped the Cosmos to the NASL championship, being voted the League's Most Valuable Player in the process. Gordon Milne enticed him to return from the glamour of New York in August 1978, tabling a successful £40,000 bid for the midfield player. It was a move which enabled Hunt to establish himself in the First Division, and marked the start of six successful years at Highfield Road.

Hunt was an accomplished midfielder, who possessed both excellent close skill and a keen eye for passing. His coolness in the centre of the park was a valuable asset in the youthful side of the early 1980s, and his name was frequently mentioned in connection with the England squad, although the call-up never came in his time at City. His only representative honour during his time at Highfield Road came as part of an unofficial England XI, who played the London FA in a testimonial match for Bill Taylor in 1982.

Over the course of his six seasons at City, Hunt made 216 appearances, and, despite a number of disagreements with the club's management, remained a first-team regular throughout. He also scored 34 goals, including 12 in 1981/82, a total only surpassed by Mark Hateley. However, in his latter years at City, Hunt was clearly unsettled and news of his sale to West Brom in March 1984 came as little surprise to supporters. Just two months after his move to The Hawthorns came the elusive England cap he had long been anticipating, with a substitute appearance in the game against Scotland in May 1984, one of just 2 England appearances he would make.

After two years with West Brom, Hunt returned to finish his League career with Aston Villa, ten years after first leaving Villa Park. After a further two years with Villa, he moved to become player-manager with non-League Willenhall Town for a season, before retiring from the game in 1989.

	League		FA Cup		League Cup			Total	
	Apps	Goals	Apps	Goals	Apps	Goals		Apps	Goals
1978/79	20 (4)	6	0	0	0	0		20 (4)	6
1979/80	34 (1)	1	0	0	3	0		37 (1)	1
1980/81	40	6	3	0	9	2		52	8
1981/82	36	9	4	3	1	0		41	12
1982/83	35	4	3	0	3	1		41	5
1983/84	13 (2)	1	4	1	1	0		18 (2)	2
TOTAL	178 (7)	27	14	4	17	3		209 (7)	34

Tommy Hutchinson
Outside left, 1972-80

In terms of longevity, few can match Tommy Hutchison's playing career, which spanned almost thirty years, from his debut for Alloa in 1965, to his retirement whilst with non-League Merthyr Tydfil, in the early 1990s. During this time, he made a mammoth 863 first-class appearances, a record only bettered by Peter Shilton. Over 300 of these matches were in the Sky Blue of Coventry, where Hutchison remains an all-time favourite for his dazzling wing performances and his ability to turn games with a flash of inspirational play. Hutchison's ball control was often breathtaking, and his dribbling skills rendered many a full-back redundant. His exciting style earned him the Player of the Year award in 1976, as well as the London Supporters' Club award in both 1978 and 1979. In a recent poll, he was voted by City fans as their all-time favourite player of the top-flight era.

Hutchison began his career with Alloa in 1965, making 68 appearances for the Scottish Second Division side before joining Blackpool three years later. He remained at Blackpool for four years, playing alongside Gordon Milne, who was, by then, nearing the end of his playing days. When Milne moved into management with Coventry in 1972, one of his first moves was to persuade his former colleague to follow him to Highfield Road. In a deal which saw Billy Rafferty move in the opposite direction, Hutchison joined the Sky Blues in October 1972. His arrival coincided with that of fellow Scot, Colin Stein, and between them they helped breathe new life into a struggling City side.

In his first four seasons, Hutchison was a model of consistency, missing a single first-team match. His performances during this time earned him international recognition, his Scotland debut coming in the 2-1 win over Czechoslovakia in September 1973. Over the next two years, he won a total of 17 caps, including 2 appearances in the 1974 World Cup finals in West Germany. His international career, however, was all too brief, and from 1975 onwards, he was never called upon again to represent his country. Many believe this was a travesty, given his continued fine form for the Sky Blues.

Hutchison continued to delight from the wing throughout his nine seasons at City, missing only a handful of matches during his stay at Highfield Road. As well as being an accomplished individual performer, he was the archetypal team player, and in his final full season was appointed as club captain. He left City in October 1980, joining Manchester City along with Bobby McDonald, in a deal which valued Hutchison at £47,000. He was thirty-three at the time of his move, and it was a reasonable judgement by City that he was a player entering the autumn of his career. With promising youngsters breaking into the first team in the form of Gary Bannister and Peter Bodak, it seemed a prudent move to allow Hutchison to move on. Had it been known how long Hutchison would continue playing, his career at City may well have lasted a good deal longer.

Hutchison remained at Manchester for two years, during which time he had the unfortunate distinction of becoming the first player to score at both ends in an FA Cup final, in the 1-1 draw with Spurs in 1981. From Maine Road, he moved to Hong Kong and spent a season with Bulova, returning to England with Burnley for the start of 1983/84. After two seasons at Turf Moor, he transferred to Swansea City, where he saw out his League career. His six years at the Vetch included his brief foray into management, his first season with the club being as a player/manager. In 1989/90, Hutchison got his first opportunity for European football, turning out for Swansea in the European Cup-winners' Cup, aged forty-two. After leaving Swansea, Hutchison moved into non-League football with Merthyr, where he finally hung up his boots.

	League		FA Cup		League Cup			Total	
	Apps	Goals	Apps	Goals	Apps	Goals		Apps	Goals
1972/73	30	2	4	1	0	0		34	3
1973/74	41	3	6	1	6	0		53	4
1974/75	42	4	3	0	1	0		46	4
1975/76	42	1	3	0	2	0		47	1
1976/77	31 (2)	3	2	1	0	0		33 (2)	4
1977/78	40	3	1	0	4	1		45	4
1978/79	42	6	2	0	1	0		45	6
1979/80	40	1	2	1	3	0		45	2
1980/81	4	1	0	0	1	1		5	2
TOTAL	312 (2)	24	23	4	18	2		353 (2)	30

Hutchison in action against Ipswich Town.

Leslie Jones
Inside forward, 1934-37

By the time of his arrival at Highfield Road, Leslie Jones was already a Welsh international with a proven goalscoring pedigree. Born on 1 July 1911 in Aberdare, South Wales, he began his career with his home town club Aberdare Athletic, joining shortly after they had lost their place in the League. He moved on to Cardiff City in 1929, where he formed a formidable strike pairing with Walter Robbins. In his five seasons at Ninian Park, he made 161 league and cup appearances netting 30 goals, including 16 in 1933/34. During his final season with the Bluebirds, his performances earned him the first of 11 Welsh caps, his debut coming in the 1-1 draw with France in Paris in May 1933. It was his stunning displays against Coventry in the Christmas games of 1933/34, which attracted the attention of Harry Storer, and at the first opportunity he swooped for the young Welshman's signature.

Jones was an immediate success at City, forming a dynamic strike partnership with Clarrie Bourton. In their first full season together they struck 59 goals, Jones finishing as top scorer with 30. His haul included no fewer than four hat-tricks: against Clapton Orient, Southend, Gillingham and Newport County. The following season, the 'Old Five' continued apace, with City roaring to the championship of the Third Division (South) on the back of the continued goalscoring form of their strike duo. This time it was Bourton who topped the scorer's charts with 26, closely followed by Jones with 19. Highlights included a hat-trick in the 6-1 drubbing of Queens Park Rangers in February, as well as two in both the 7-1 victory over Newport County and the 8-1 success at home to Crystal Palace.

By this stage, Jones was attracting the attention of higher division clubs, and offers for the Welsh striker began coming in. The most significant of these came from Spurs who were willing to pay £7,000, a princely sum in the 1930s, for Jones' services. City refused, however, viewing Jones as a key figure in their assault on the Second Division. In their first season at this higher level, City finished eighth, with Jones scoring 10 in their efforts. The following year Coventry were looking like true promotion contenders, topping the table by November. Jones' early season form had been excellent so it was a bombshell for the City faithful when his transfer to Arsenal was announced in the same month. The fee was £2,000, plus Scottish inside right Bobby Davidson, a player who had greatly impressed Storer. Financially, City were looking to recoup the fees recently spent on Tony MacPhee and George Taylor and so Jones' sale, although a gamble, was viewed as a necessity. Whilst Jones went on to win a First Division Championship medal with the Gunners that season, Coventry's promotion hopes floundered, eventually finishing fourth and missing out on the promised land of the First Division. In the eyes of many, the sale of Jones was the single greatest contributing factor to the failure to win promotion, and the question was oft-asked what might have been had it not been for the departure of one of the club's most consistent performers at such a crucial time.

Jones remained with the Gunners until 1946, playing regularly during the Second World War, as well as 'guesting' for no fewer than thirteen other clubs, including Coventry. He made nine appearances for the wartime City side, with his farewell appearance coming in the 3-2 defeat against Birmingham in September 1945. Jones also made 5 wartime international appearances for Wales, to add to his peacetime caps.

| | League | | FA Cup | | | Total | |
	Apps	Goals	Apps	Goals		Apps	Goals
1933/34	16	10	0	0		16	10
1934/35	41	27	3	3		44	30
1935/36	32	19	0	0		32	19
1936/37	37	9	3	1		40	10
1937/38	12	4	0	0		12	4
TOTAL	138	69	6	4		144	73

Eli Juggins
Defender, 1907-14

Eli Juggins was a formidable force in the City defence during the late Birmingham League and early Southern League days. Although standing at only 5ft 9in, Juggins was built like the proverbial carthorse, weighing in at over 14 stone. Combined with the fact that he played a very physical game, it is not difficult to see why he was treated with a healthy respect by opposing forwards! In his youth, Juggins played in the Walsall and Wolverhampton Junior Leagues, before signing for Darlaston as a seventeen-year-old. In 1904, after less than two months with Darlaston, he was signed by Wolverhampton Wanderers, and it was whilst at Wolves that he converted to a defensive role, after initially playing as an outside right.

After three years at Molineux, Juggins became involved in a dispute with the club over payments he felt he was due. Consequently, he left Wolves, and was snapped up by Coventry, who were eager to strengthen the side in preparation for their application to join the Southern League. Juggins was a regular throughout his first season, proving to be a steadfast and reliable defender, who also filled in as centre forward when required. He featured heavily in the lengthy cup run, playing in each of the 9 ties, and scoring 4 goals, as City reached the first round proper, before bowing out to Crystal Palace.

Juggins remained a first-choice full-back through the first season of Southern League football in 1908/09, playing 29 matches and scoring twice. However, over the next three seasons, his appearances became more infrequent, and he was primarily a squad player. As his playing days drew to an end, he became involved in the training side at the club, initially as an assistant to James McIntyre, and then upon McIntyre's departure in 1912, as trainer. He played three final games for City in November 1913, bringing his total appearances to 111, before leaving the club at the end of the season and moving to Southampton. In 1919, he returned to City for a spell as ground superintendent.

	Birmingham League		FA Cup			Total	
	Apps	Goals	Apps	Goals		Apps	Goals
1907/08	30	1	9	4		39	5

	Southern League		FA Cup			Total	
	Apps	Goals	Apps	Goals		Apps	Goals
1908/09	28	2	1	0		29	2
1909/10	20	0	1	0		21	0
1910/11	16	0	1	0		17	0
1911/12	2	0	0	0		2	0
1913/14	2	0	1	0		3	0
TOTAL	98	3	13	4		111	7

Mick Kearns
Defender, 1955-68

It was Jesse Carver who first spotted Mick Kearns playing for local team Stockingford Villa, bringing him to Highfield Road in September 1955. It was two years, however, before Kearns got his opportunity in the first team, making his debut in the 3-0 defeat at Bournemouth in September 1957. It wasn't until the following year that he became a first-team regular, helping City win promotion from the Fourth Division at the first attempt. During his first few seasons as a regular, Kearns played predominantly as a wing-half, before switching to a full-back role during the Jimmy Hill era. He proved capable in any of the positions he was required to play, and although often an unsung hero, was a vital member of the team through the early-to-mid-1960s.

Kearns missed relatively few games during his ten years in the first team, despite being troubled with recurrent knee injuries – which often necessitated pain-killing injections before games. He was a valued member of the teams which won promotion from the Third Division in 1964 and the Second in 1967. His service to City earned him a testimonial in 1967, jointly with George Curtis; 25,000 fans paid their thanks to two of City's greatest servants, as Coventry beat Liverpool 2-1.

Coventry's first season in the top flight proved to be Kearns' last for the club, as his troublesome knee complaint finally necessitated his retirement from the game. He made his final appearance in February 1968, in the FA Cup tie with Tranmere, bringing to a close a career which had seen him make 382 appearances for the Sky Blues. He remained living locally, running the family's bingo hall in Nuneaton, and returned to Highfield Road in 1986 as a coach, and, later, chief scout.

	League		FA Cup		League Cup		Total	
	Apps	Goals	Apps	Goals	Apps	Goals	Apps	Goals
1957/58	3	0	0	0	-	-	3	0
1958/59	32	2	2	0	-	-	34	2
1959/60	31	3	0	0	-	-	31	3
1960/61	40	2	3	0	1	1	44	3
1961/62	26	2	0	0	0	0	26	2
1962/63	36	2	9	0	1	0	46	2
1963/64	42	0	2	1	1	0	45	1
1964/65	36	0	1	0	4	0	41	0
1965/66	40	2	4	0	4	0	48	2
1966/67	41	1	1	0	3	0	45	1
1967/68	17	0	2	0	0	0	19	0
TOTAL	344	14	24	1	14	1	382	16

Brian Kilcline
Centre half, 1984-91

Brian Kilcline made an imposing figure in the City defence. Six foot four, with 'Viking' looks, his uncompromising, physical style of play made him a fearsome opponent. Whilst never the most naturally skilled of players, his commitment and sheer determination was renowned, and he led by example as team captain. His greatest day came in the Cup Final win in 1987, when he hobbled up the Wembley steps to receive City's first major trophy, after leaving the field injured in the second-half.

'Killer' began his career at Notts County, where he signed as a professional in 1979. Ever-present in the 1981 promotion-winning side, he was a regular up until joining the Sky Blues in June 1984. Once at Highfield Road, he quickly struck up an excellent partnership with Trevor Peake, which formed the mainstay of the defence throughout the late 1980s.

Upon Stuart Pearce's departure, Kilcline took over as penalty taker, with his self-confessed strategy of 'hitting them as hard as he could' serving City well. Until his final season, Killer's record from the spot was excellent, adding to his prowess from free-kicks. He scored some valuable goals, perhaps none more so than in the penultimate game of 1984/85, when his 85th-minute winner against Luton offered the Sky Blues a First Division survival lifeline.

His major downfall during his stay at City was his proneness for picking up relatively minor injuries, which caused him to miss significant portions of a number of his six seasons with the club. However, despite this, he made over 200 appearances, scoring 35 goals in his time at Highfield Road.

Kilcline left City for Oldham Athletic in July 1991 in a deal worth £400,000. His stay with the Latics was brief, however, making only 10 appearances before becoming Kevin Keegan's first signing for Newcastle in March 1992. He was part of the Newcastle side which won promotion to the top flight, scoring an invaluable 12 goals in the promotion season. After eighteen months at St James' Park, he moved to Swindon for £90,000. After a spell at Mansfield Town, his playing career ended with a flourish, helping Halifax Town to the Conference Championship and promotion to the League in the 1997/98 season.

	League		FA Cup		League Cup		Other		Total	
	Apps	Goals	Apps	Goals	Apps	Goals	Apps	Goals	Apps	Goals
1984/85	26	2	2	0	1 (1)	0	0	0	29 (1)	2
1985/86	32	7	1	1	4	1	2	0	39	9
1986/87	29	3	6	0	2	1	0	0	37	4
1987/88	28	8	2	1	0	0	4	0	34	9
1988/89	33	4	1	0	3	1	1	0	38	5
1989/90	11	1	0	0	4	1	1	0	16	2
1990/91	14	3	3	1	2	0	0	0	19	4
TOTAL	173	28	15	3	16 (1)	4	8	0	212 (1)	35

Roy Kirk
Defender, 1952-60

Roy Kirk began his playing career in his home town of Bolsover in Derbyshire, playing as a utility man for the Bolsover Colliery team. After a brief spell with Luton Town, he was spotted by Leeds United and signed for the Elland Road club in August 1948. However, his chances at Leeds were limited by the consistency of John Charles, and in his four years at the club, he only made 39 appearances.

In March 1952, Harry Storer brought Kirk to Highfield Road for a fee of £10,000. Storer was looking to breathe new life into an ageing City side and rescue City from the precarious position that saw them facing relegation to the Third Division. Whilst Kirk proved to be an excellent purchase, adequately filling the centre half position that had been vacated by George Mason, his arrival did little to change the course of the campaign, and his 9 games that season proved to be City's last in the Second Division before relegation.

Over the next eight seasons, Kirk was a constant in the City defence, providing stability during a time of constant change at the club. He missed very few games throughout his City career, and for three of his eight seasons was an ever present in the side. Primarily, he played at centre half, but also had spells in both full-back positions, and demonstrated the versatility to adapt to whatever role was required of him.

Kirk can claim to have scored perhaps the most unlikely of goals for City, when he netted against Northampton Town in November 1954. He shot from the penalty area and looped the ball over the head of ex-City 'keeper, Alf Woods, and into the net. What was amazing was that it was Coventry's own penalty area that he struck the ball from – some eighty yards from the Northampton goal! Two months previously, he had been involved in another unlikely occurrence, when he scored a brace of own goals in the 2-0 defeat against Leyton Orient.

After nearly 350 games for City, Kirk moved to Cambridge United in the close season of 1960. After four years as a player at the Abbey Stadium, he took on the role of manager in 1964, a position he held for two years, before leaving the game.

| | League | | FA Cup | | Total | |
	Apps	Goals	Apps	Goals	Apps	Goals
1951/52	9	0	0	0	9	0
1952/53	40	1	3	0	43	1
1953/54	46	2	1	0	47	2
1954/55	46	0	4	1	50	1
1955/56	45	0	1	0	46	0
1956/57	39	0	0	0	39	0
1957/58	33	0	2	0	35	0
1958/59	46	3	2	0	48	3
1959/60	26	0	2	0	28	0
TOTAL	330	6	15	1	345	7

Billy Lake
Forward, 1928-39

Prior to the Second World War, Billy Lake was Coventry's longest serving player, spending eleven years at the club between 1928 and 1939. Born in Birmingham in 1908, he began his career with local non-League side Yardley White Star, before signing for Walsall. Lake's father was on the board of directors at Fellows Park at the time and undoubtedly played a part in giving the young striker his break. He spent two years at Walsall, during which time he made 27 appearances for the Saddlers and scored 8 goals. In November 1929, new City manager James McIntyre brought Lake to Highfield Road hoping the young forward could rejuvenate his City side, who had been struggling in the southern section of the Third Division. Lake made his debut in the 1-3 reverse at Queens Park Rangers, and quickly formed a devastating strike pairing with Jimmy Loughlin. In their first full season as City's forward line, they amassed 47 goals with Lake providing 17, including his first hat-trick for the club in the 3-1 victory over Norwich in November 1929. The following season it was Lake's turn to be top scorer, his tally of 24 being his highest single season total during his City career. Highlights included four in the 5-1 victory over Bristol Rovers in March 1931 and a brace in the exciting 6-4 win against Newport County in November 1930.

In June 1931, Harry Storer took over as City manager, and Lake proved to be the one player who successfully made the transition from the McIntyre era. The arrival of Clarrie Bourton and Jock Lauderdale in time for the start of the 1931/32 season cemented a forward line that was formidable, and together they set a record for the number of League goals scored by Coventry in any one season – a mammoth 108. Although over-shadowed by the scoring exploits of his fellow strikers, Lake's contribution of 15 goals continued his average of a goal every other game – a record he maintained until his retirement.

Lake continued as a regular in the City forward line for the next two seasons, scoring 20 and 17 respectively. However, he lost his place on the arrival of Welsh international Leslie Jones in January 1934, and his made only sporadic appearances from then onwards. His scoring record, however, never deteriorated – whenever called upon, Lake showed the attacking pace and flair that had made him so prolific. He enjoyed a particularly purple patch in early 1938, netting seven in three games, including all four in the 4-1 victory over Luton Town.

With the outbreak of the Second World War, Lake announced his retirement from the game, aged just thirty-one. In his 245 games for City, he had scored 123 goals, a total only ever bettered by Clarrie Bourton himself.

	League		FA Cup			Total	
	Apps	Goals	Apps	Goals		Apps	Goals
1928/29	7	2	0	0		7	2
1929/30	36	15	4	2		40	17
1930/31	41	23	3	1		44	24
1931/32	28	14	2	1		30	15
1932/33	35	18	4	2		39	20
1933/34	31	16	2	1		33	17
1934/35	12	9	0	0		12	9
1935/36	18	4	1	1		19	5
1936/37	2	2	3	2		5	4
1937/38	7	7	0	0		7	7
1938/39	9	3	0	0		9	3
TOTAL	226	113	19	10		245	123

1933/34 Coventry City line-up. From left to right, back row: Davison, Morgan, Brown, Klimpton (trainer), Boileau, Pearson, Mason. Middle row: Bacon, Blytheway, Wilmot, Storer (manager), Bisby, Baker, Lax. Front row: White, Lauderdale, Bourton, Lake, Richards.

Jock Lauderdale
Forward, 1931-36

As his name would suggest, Jock Lauderdale hailed from north of the Border, having been born in Dumfries on 27 November 1908. He began his career in his native Scotland in the mid-1920s, turning out for Parkhead, Third Lanark, Stenhousemuir and Queen of the South between 1925 and 1929. In October 1929, he was signed by Harry Evans for First Division Blackpool, but he made only 21 appearances in two years with the Seasiders before Harry Storer brought him to Highfield Road for a fee of £270.

Lauderdale made a scoring debut in the 3-5 reverse at Fulham in the opening match of 1931/32, and he immediately struck up an excellent partnership with Clarrie Bourton in the City forward line, as the team entered their most successful period to date. Goals came in abundance during the early 1930s and, in his first season, Lauderdale weighed in with 19 of a record 108 League goals scored by City. He also proved more than able to set up opportunities for others, and his skilful play from inside-right provided many chances for Bourton, in particular, to feed off. The City faithful loved Jock, and christened the era that of the 'Old Five' in recognition of the number of times Coventry put five goals past the opposition.

Over the next four seasons Lauderdale continued as a regular in the City front line, scoring 44 more goals. He was a fundamental part of the Third Division (South) championship winning side of 1935/36, making 23 appearances and scoring 11 goals towards the cause. His performances had not gone unnoticed by rival clubs, and during this time a number of significant offers for his services were received, including a £2,000 bid from Liverpool in 1934. However, City were keen to hold on to their man and turned down all approaches.

Lauderdale eventually lost his place in the side to Bill McDonald a few games into City's Second Division campaign of 1936/37. He moved on in November of 1936, signing for Northampton Town for £1,700. By this stage, Lauderdale was in the twilight of his career and his time at Northampton was plagued by injuries. He remained with the Cobblers for three years, making 49 appearances and scoring 9 goals before transferring to non-league Nuneaton Borough in 1939. During the War he made the occasional appearance back at Highfield Road, guesting for Coventry. In total he made five wartime appearances for City, with his final game the 1-0 defeat against Walsall in August 1942. He remained in Coventry after retiring up until his death in 1965, aged fifty-eight.

| | League | | FA Cup | | Total | |
	Apps	Goals	Apps	Goals	Apps	Goals
1931/32	42	19	2	0	44	19
1932/33	41	15	4	0	45	15
1933/34	40	11	2	1	42	12
1934/35	21	4	1	2	22	6
1935/36	23	11	2	0	25	11
1936/37	4	0	0	0	4	0
TOTAL	171	60	11	3	182	63

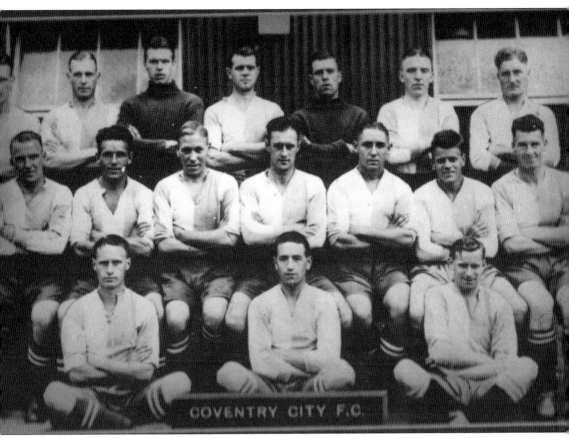

Coventry City 1935/36. From left to right, back row: G. Mason, R. Brook, W. Morgan, V. Brown, H. Pearson, C. McCaughey, H. Boileau. Middle row: C. Bisby, G. McNestry, J. Lauderdale, C. Bourton, L. Jones, A. Fitton, H. Webb. Front row: W. Frith, W. Lake, F. Liddle.

Arthur Lightening

Goalkeeper, 1958-62

In December 1958, Coventry manager Billy Frith made one of his most astute pieces of transfer business, when he completed the dual signing of Arthur Lightening and Ron Farmer from Nottingham Forest. The combined fee of £6,000 proved to be a bargain, for a duo who would go on to make almost 500 appearances between them, and who helped lift City from their lowest ebb in the basement division of English football.

A South African, Lightening had come to England at the behest of Forest in 1956. However, in his two years at the City Ground, he found himself unable to break into the first team, and it was whilst playing for Forest reserves that he was spotted by Frith. Impressed with his agility and strength, Frith put Lightening straight into the City team, his debut coming in the 4-1 victory over Hartlepools United in December 1958. He was ever present throughout the rest of the season, as Coventry won promotion from the Fourth Division at the first attempt.

Over the next four years, Lightening became a firm favourite with the City fans, continuing Coventry's tradition of excellent 'keepers. His performances earned him favourable comparisons with recent City hero, Reg Matthews – praise indeed, when one considers the high regard in which Matthews was still held. He remained the first-choice 'keeper until 1962, amassing a total of 160 appearances, before the shock decision to sell Lightening to Middlesborough was announced to stunned City fans in August 1962. Many questioned the logic of Jimmy Hill's decision to dispense with the services of a 'keeper in the best of form, when an obvious replacement of a similar calibre was not forthcoming. A clue to Hill's reasoning may have come a few weeks later, when Lightening was to appear in a Coventry court, charged with receiving stolen property. Whatever the true reason, the deal was completed and, for a fee of £11,000, Lightening departed City for Ayresome Park.

His career at Middlesborough was brief and, within a year, Lightening had returned to South Africa and brought to an end his time in English football. Returning initially to attend his brother's funeral, he made the decision to remain permanently in his homeland. He remained in his homeland until his death in late 2001 at the age of sixty-five.

	League		FA Cup		League Cup		Total	
	Apps	Goals	Apps	Goals	Apps	Goals	Apps	Goals
1958/59	25	0	0	0	-	-	25	0
1959/60	46	0	2	0	-	-	48	0
1960/61	33	0	3	0	2	0	38	0
1961/62	42	0	2	0	1	0	45	0
1962/63	4	0	0	0	0	0	4	0
TOTAL	150	0	7	0	3	0	160	0

Norman Lockhart
Outside left, 1947-52

Norman Lockhart already had a successful career in Ireland behind him when he joined Coventry in October 1947. While playing for Linfield, he had won two Irish Cups in consecutive years (1945 and 1946), and had been a losing finalist in 1944. He had also won the first of 8 caps for Northern Ireland, having made his debut in the harrowing 7-2 defeat at the hands of England in 1946. His career began with Irish junior side, Windsor Star, from where he moved on to Distillery in 1940. Two years later, he transferred to Linfield, where he spent four profitable years, prior to moving to the English League with Swansea Town in October 1946. His stay at the Vetch was brief, but sufficient to alert Coventry manager Billy Frith to his talents, and he was signed for Coventry in October 1947. A debut in the home draw against Bury in the same month began a City career that lasted five years, and almost 200 matches.

Lockhart was a pacy winger, who had the ability to provide pinpoint accurate crosses, as well as having a sharp eye for goal himself. His time at Highfield Road coincided with a period of decline, and eventual relegation, for City – but this did not detract from his individual performances, a fact highlighted by his recall to international duty in March 1950, some three-and-a-half years after his previous call-up. Throughout his five years with City, Lockhart was a first-team regular, never playing fewer than 30 games in any of his five seasons. In terms of goalscoring, his most successful campaign came in his last full season with the club (1951/52), when he notched 17 goals and was City's top scorer. It was the only year his tally made double figures, though he managed a total of 44 during his Coventry career.

Shortly after Coventry were relegated to the Third Division, Lockhart left Highfield Road for Aston Villa, for a fee of £15,500. He spent five years at Villa Park, making 73 appearances, before moving to Bury, where he ended his career.

	League		FA Cup		Total	
	Apps	Goals	Apps	Goals	Apps	Goals
1947/48	31	6	2	1	33	7
1948/49	31	5	1	0	32	5
1949/50	32	7	0	0	32	7
1950/51	38	7	1	0	39	7
1951/52	42	15	3	2	45	17
1952/53	8	1	0	0	8	1
TOTAL	182	41	7	3	189	44

George Lowrie
Centre forward, 1939-48

George Lowrie signed for Coventry at the least opportune time, making his debut in the last peacetime match before the outbreak of the Second World War. His career had begun at Swansea Town, signing when only fifteen years old. He spent three seasons at the Vetch Field, but was never able to break into the first team and transferred to Burnley in December 1937. After only four games in the side, he came to the attention of City manager Harry Storer, who paid £1,750 to bring him to Highfield Road. Recognising Lowrie's attacking potential, Storer saw him as possibly the final piece in the jigsaw for a City side who were missing a prolific scorer since the departure of Clarrie Bourton and were pushing for promotion to the First Division. His debut came in the 4-2 victory over Barnsley on 2 September 1939 in the aborted 1939/40 Second Division campaign. The outbreak of war, however, saw the suspension of the Football League and Lowrie's career was 'put on hold' at the age of only nineteen.

He continued to play for City in wartime matches, notching up 65 goals in 98 appearances and he 'guested' for Northampton Town, Nottingham Forest and Bristol City. His wartime performances, warranted his first representative honours, with appearances in 8 wartime internationals for Wales.

Upon the resumption of peacetime football, Lowrie made a blistering start to his City career 'second-time around'. In 1946/7, he netted 29 goals in 36 appearances including five hat-tricks. The following season was started the way in which the previous had left off, with a four-goal haul in the opening match against Luton, which was followed a week later by a hat-trick away at Brentford. By now, Lowrie was attracting the attention of a number of first division clubs, and it was only a matter of time before City, who were struggling financially, had to cash in on their main asset. He remained at City until March of 1947/48, during which time he netted 18 goals in 22 games and also received the first three of his four Welsh caps.

It was Second Division promotion contenders Newcastle United who eventually secured Lowrie's signature for a club record fee received of £18,500. His time on Tyneside, however, was frustrating, with only twelve appearances during his eighteen month spell. In September 1949 he transferred to Bristol City for £10,000, before returning to Coventry in early 1952 to help with their struggle against relegation. Lowrie was past his prime by this stage and his tally of 3 goals in 12 games was not enough to stave off the drop. He remained at City for their return season in Third Division (South), playing 15 further games, before ending his career in the Southern League with Lovells Athletic.

| | League | | FA Cup | | Total | |
	Apps	Goals	Apps	Goals	Apps	Goals
1946/47	34	26	2	3	36	29
1947/48	22	18	0	0	22	18
1951/52	12	3	0	0	12	3
1952/53	15	9	0	0	15	9
TOTAL	83	56	2	3	85	59

Gary McAllister
Midfield, 1996-2000

By the time he arrived at Highfield Road, Gary McAllister was already one of the most highly respected players in the domestic game. With Leeds, he had been a crucial member of the 1992 Championship-winning side and their European campaign the following year. On the international scene, he had captained his country through Euro 1996 and already had 44 caps to his name. He was renowned as a midfield master, who could control and dictate the game from the centre of the park. His signing for Coventry in 1996 was seen as evidence that the Sky Blues were, at last, competing to recruit players of the finest calibre, and hopes were high, despite manager Ron Atkinson's disappointing first season. At £3 million, McAllister was Coventry City's most expensive signing to date. However, in his first season at Highfield Road, he failed to live up to his billing and his performances were disappointing. In only brief spells did City fans enjoy McAllister at his best and there was evident frustration from the terraces. The following season, injury meant that McAllister only featured in 14 League games for City, and fears that his career had gone into terminal decline were mounting. Such fears were to prove totally unfounded and, in his final seasons at Highfield Road, McAllister was to shine.

In 1998/99, McAllister brought to an end his international career, retiring as captain due to the barracking he received in the defeat against the Czechs in March 1999. His country's loss was City's gain, as McAllister's form for Coventry improved dramatically. By far his finest season for the Sky Blues came in 1999/2000, when he was no less than magnificent in City's midfield. It was a season when Coventry were christened 'the entertainers', with the Moroccans, Hadji and Chippo, showing flair in abundance and Robbie Keane dazzling up front. McAllister was the kingpin of the team, dominating the midfield and proving to be one of the classiest performers in the Premiership. His attacking skills were more evident than ever before, as he ended the season as the club's top scorer with 13 goals. Deservedly, he won the Player of the Year award in what was to be his final campaign for the club. In the summer of 2000, out-of-contract McAllister moved on to Liverpool on a Bosman free transfer. At thirty-five, he wanted an opportunity to play for one of the 'bigger' clubs, and Gerard Houllier snapped him up. He has continued to be a revelation at Anfield, helping the side to both domestic trophies and the UEFA Cup in his first year. Champions League qualification offers McAllister another chance for European glory in 2001/02.

	League		FA Cup		League Cup			Total	
	Apps	Goals	Apps	Goals	Apps	Goals		Apps	Goals
1996/97	38	6	4	0	4	1		46	7
1997/98	14	0	0	0	4	2		18	2
1998/99	29	3	3	1	1	0		33	4
1999/2000	38	11	3	0	2	2		43	13
TOTAL	119	20	10	1	11	5		140	26

Bobby McDonald
Left-back, 1976-80

Bobby McDonald began his career with Aston Villa, where he progressed through the youth ranks and appeared in a FA Youth Cup final in 1973. In 1975, he won a League Cup-winners' medal with Villa, but by the following year was unsettled by his lack of first-team appearances. Gordon Milne brought him to City in the August 1976, for what was to prove a bargain fee of £40,000. He fitted in immediately at left-back, where the departure of Chris Cattlin to Brighton had left a void. Over the next four seasons, McDonald was a permanent fixture in the City side. Indeed, from his debut against Bristol City in August 1976, he made 178 consecutive League and cup appearances.

A tough-tackling full-back, McDonald also demonstrated himself well able to make overlapping runs down the flank, and added an extra dimension to attacking play. He also scored some memorable goals, perhaps his finest coming against Chelsea in September 1978. After picking up the ball just inside his own half, McDonald embarked on a superb solo run, before slotting the ball past Peter Bonnetti for City's equalizer. In 1978/79, his performances earned him the Player of the Year award, a testimony to his consistency in the Sky Blues' defence. At his peak, he was pushing for international honours, but with Willie Donachie incumbent in the left-back slot for Scotland, the call-up never came.

In April 1980, McDonald was dropped from the starting line-up for the first time since his arrival. He played only two further matches at the start of 1980/81, before being transferred, along with Tommy Hutchison, to Manchester City. It is unfortunate that he offended many Coventry fans on his arrival at Manchester, by slating his former club as 'lacking ambition.' In his first season at Maine Road, he appeared in the FA Cup final, coming away with a losers' medal, after Manchester City were beaten in a replay by Spurs.

McDonald remained at Maine Road for three seasons, leaving shortly after their relegation to the Second Division, following a breach of club discipline. He moved on to Oxford United, where he was part of the side that briefly reached the top flight. In 1987, he transferred to Leeds United, and finally ended his League career a year later, with a loan spell at Wolves. He continued playing at non-League level for some years, appearing for VS Rugby, Nuneaton Borough, and Worcester City, among others.

	League		FA Cup		League Cup		Total	
	Apps	Goals	Apps	Goals	Apps	Goals	Apps	Goals
1976/77	39	1	2	1	3	0	44	2
1977/78	42	5	1	0	4	0	47	5
1978/79	42	4	2	0	1	0	45	4
1979/80	37	4	2	0	3	0	42	4
1980/81	1	0	0	0	0 (1)	0	1 (1)	0
TOTAL	161	14	7	1	11 (1)	0	179 (1)	15

Martin McDonnell
Defender, 1949-55

Martin McDonnell's football career began at Goodison Park, signing for Everton as a wartime player in 1942. However, he was soon called up for military service, and his career with the Toffeemen was forcibly interrupted. When peacetime football restarted in 1946, McDonnell was granted a free transfer and joined neighbours Southport, where he spent a solitary season. In October 1947, he joined Birmingham City, who were managed at the time by Harry Storer, and it would be the first of three occasions on which Storer would sign McDonnell at various clubs.

McDonnell enjoyed success at St Andrews, featuring in the side that won the Second Division championship in 1948. However, his outings in the First Division were limited and in May 1949, Storer, who had returned to the Coventry City hotseat, signed McDonnell for a second time. The fee of £10,000 proved to be money well spent, as McDonnell enjoyed the most productive and consistent years of his career at Highfield Road.

His debut for City came in October 1949, in the 2-1 win over Cardiff City, a game in which McDonnell featured as City's right-back. He continued to play as a full-back until early 1950, when he switched to what would become his customary position of centre half. Over the next five seasons, McDonnell proved to be a more than adequate replacement for the long-serving George Mason, and showed himself to be a solid and reliable player during a difficult time for the Bantams. His service was rewarded in 1951 with the captaincy of the side, an honour he held periodically during the next four years.

In April 1955, City's acting manager Charlie Elliott decided that the City defence needed restructuring and he switched Roy Kirk from his left-back role into the centre half position, dropping McDonnell from the side. It was a move that signalled the end of McDonnell's career at Highfield Road, after six years and 245 appearances. It is a mark of his consistency at City to note that from his debut in 1949, he missed only 11 first-team matches, until he was dropped in 1955.

In the close season of 1955, he was allowed to leave the club, and was once again signed by Harry Storer, this time for Derby County. He stayed with the Rams for three years, helping them to the Third Division (North) championship in 1957, before moving onto Crewe Alexandra in July 1958. After ending his career with Crewe, he returned to live in Coventry.

	League		FA Cup		Total	
	Apps	Goals	Apps	Goals	Apps	Goals
1949/50	28	0	1	0	29	0
1950/51	42	0	1	0	43	0
1951/52	39	0	3	0	42	0
1952/53	42	0	3	0	45	0
1953/54	44	0	1	0	45	0
1954/55	37	0	4	0	41	0
TOTAL	232	0	13	0	245	0

Lloyd McGrath
Midfield, 1982-93

Lloyd McGrath was a terrier in the City midfield, an uncompromising player who was renowned for his tough tackling and his man-marking. He was a great favourite of the City fans, who recognized his commitment and valued his ability to render even the most skilled of opponents redundant with his vigorous marking. Undoubtedly, his greatest moment for Coventry came in the 1987 FA Cup final, when his injury-time cross-shot was deflected past Ray Clemence for City's winning goal. It was a fitting way to mark McGrath's 100th appearance for the Sky Blues.

McGrath signed professional forms at Coventry in December 1982, overcoming a serious injury whilst still in the youth ranks, to progress on to the first team in 1984. Initially a centre half, McGrath made his debut against Southampton in what was to be City's worst post-war defeat, losing 8-2. In his third game, City again capitulated, this time letting in six against Chelsea. Shortly afterwards, McGrath moved to his customary midfield role, and, from December 1984, he became a regular in the heart of the City line-up. Probably his best season for the Sky Blues came in 1986/87, with McGrath registering some outstanding performances in the revitalized side under Sillett and Curtis. 1986 also saw McGrath earn his only international honours, his solitary under-21 cap coming in England's game against Denmark.

After the FA Cup success, McGrath was plagued with a series of injuries which severely restricted his appearances. It was not until 1991/92 that he was able to enjoy an injury-free season, looking a revitalized player in his 47 appearances that campaign. In 1993, his service to Coventry was honoured with a testimonial year, in what was to be his final season for the club. After 246 games for the Sky Blues, he moved on in early 1993, first for a spell in Hong Kong, and later to Portsmouth, where he ended his playing career.

	League		FA Cup		League Cup		Other		Total	
	Apps	Goals	Apps	Goals	Apps	Goals	Apps	Goals	Apps	Goals
1983/84	1	0	0	0	0	0	0	0	1	0
1984/85	22 (1)	0	2	0	0	0	0	0	24 (1)	0
1985/86	32	0	1	0	4	0	0	0	37	0
1986/87	30	3	4	0	5	0	0	0	39	3
1987/88	17	0	2	0	3	0	3	0	25	0
1988/89	6 (2)	0	1	0	0	0	1	0	8 (2)	0
1989/90	12 (1)	0	1	0	2	0	0	0	15 (1)	0
1990/91	12 (2)	0	2	0	1	0	1	0	16 (2)	0
1991/92	38 (2)	1	2	0	4	1	1	0	45 (2)	2
1992/93	20 (5)	0	1	0	2	0	0	0	23 (5)	0
TOTAL	190(13)	4	16	0	21	1	6	0	233(13)	5

Ken McPherson
Centre forward, 1955-58

Ken McPherson was a centre forward in the mould of yesteryear: a powerfully-built striker who played a traditionally English type of game, using his strength and aerial ability to dominate opposition defences. He began his playing career as an amateur with Hartlepools United, before moving on to Notts County in 1950. From Meadow Lane, he joined Middlesbrough in 1953, for the sizeable fee of £15,000. However, he faced stiff competition for the forward places while at Ayresome Park, and proved unable to dislodge Wilf Mannion and Charlie Wayman as the first-choice strikeforce. Consequently, when City offered £8,000 for his services in December 1955, Middlesbrough were happy to accept, and McPherson duly became a Coventry City player.

At Highfield Road, he proved an instant success, with his bustling style of play adding much needed strength to the City forward line. He slotted into the first team immediately, scoring on his debut and netting 13 in the 1955/56 season. The following campaign proved to be McPherson's only full season as a regular in the first team. He lead the forward line with style, and was top scorer with 23 goals in 41 games. It was to be the pinnacle of his days as a Coventry player, as the following year saw the goals dry up, and McPherson feature only sporadically during the latter half of the campaign. The arrival of Ray Straw, in November 1957, effectively brought McPherson's time at Highfield Road to an end, and he left to joining Newport County in the close season of 1955. In all, he played 91 games for Coventry and scored 40 goals, averaging just under a goal every other game.

McPherson went on to be a success at Newport County, continuing his excellent scoring record with 51 goals in 128 League games for the Somerton Park side. After three years in South Wales, he spent the summer of 1961 playing in America with the New York Americans, before returning to join Swindon Town in a £2,550 deal. He ended his playing days with Swindon, converting to centre half for his final four seasons, before hanging up his boots in 1965.

	League		FA Cup		Total	
	Apps	Goals	Apps	Goals	Apps	Goals
1955/56	25	13	0	0	25	13
1956/57	40	22	1	1	41	23
1957/58	24	3	1	1	25	4
TOTAL	89	38	2	2	91	40

Ernie Machin
Midfield, 1962-72

A mere £50 was all that it took for Jimmy Hill to acquire the services of Ernie Machin in March 1962. Unfortunately, he did the young midfielder no favours, by commenting that he had signed him because he had 'liked the colour of his eyes' – ensuring that Machin would have to work twice as hard to justify himself and to overcome the stigma of being the manager's 'blue-eyed boy'! He was an ebullient player, who was constantly in the hub of the action. Predominantly playing at as a left-sided inside forward, Machin also proved capable of scoring important goals, amassing a total of 39 during his ten years with the club. He was a vital member of the team throughout the late 1960s, helping City achieve and maintain their top flight status against difficult odds.

Machin had to wait a year after signing from Nelson, before he made his debut in the 2-0 win over Millwall in April 1963. He played a further 5 games in the 1962/63 season, and was beginning to establish himself as a regular the following year, when disaster struck. During an excellent run of form, which had seen him tipped for an imminent England under-23 call-up, he suffered a serious knee injury in the game against Watford in October 1963. The injury kept him out of action for almost a full year, and would be a recurrent problem throughout the rest of his career. It was not until 1965/66 that Machin was able to re-establish himself in the first team, and join the push for promotion to the First Division.

The Second Division championship campaign saw Machin have one of his finest seasons for the Sky Blues, scoring 11 goals, including the crucial equalizer in the championship decider against Wolves. He made a smooth transition to top-flight football, and was a key figure in the early years of consolidation in the First Division. However, by the early 1970s, his knee problems recurred, and he found it increasingly difficult to maintain the pace and fitness required in the top division. In December 1972, he moved on to Plymouth Argyle for a sum of £35,000. A year later, he returned to Highfield Road for his testimonial match, awarded in recognition of the fine service he gave to the club. Over 4,000 fans turned out to give their thanks and watch City draw 1-1 with Aston Villa.

Machin stayed with Plymouth for two seasons, before moving to Brighton for his final two years in League football. He briefly made a return to Highfield Road to act as youth team coach, before leaving the game altogether.

	League Apps	Goals	FA Cup Apps	Goals	League Cup Apps	Goals	Other Apps	Goals	Total Apps	Goals
1962/63	6	0	0	0	0	0	0	0	6	0
1963/64	17	3	0	0	1	1	0	0	18	4
1964/65	14	4	1	0	2	0	0	0	17	4
1965/66	38 (1)	4	2	0	3	2	0	0	43 (1)	6
1966/67	34	11	1	0	1	0	0	0	36	11
1967/68	40	4	3	0	1	1	0	0	44	5
1968/69	41	5	2	1	4	0	0	0	47	6
1969/70	15 (1)	1	2	0	1	0	0	0	18 (1)	1
1970/71	24	0	1	0	1	1	2	0	28	1
1971/72	15	1	1	0	0	0	0	0	16	1
1972/73	11	0	0	0	2	0	1	0	14	0
TOTAL	255 (2)	33	13	1	16	5	3	0	287 (2)	39

Neil Martin
Centre forward, 1968-71

After excelling at schoolboy rugby, Neil Martin began his football career with Scottish non-League side Tranent Juniors when he was sixteen. His talent soon showed and he began alerting scouts from the Scottish League: indeed he was offered a trial at Rangers, but declined after seeing a friend languish in their third team. In 1959, he joined Alloa, where he remained for two seasons before transferring to Queen of the South. His time at Palmerston Park was productive, with Martin scoring regularly, notching 35 in his best season for the South. Hibernian shelled out £7,000 to bring Martin to Easter Road in July 1963, where he was selected to represent the Scottish League side. His ability in the air made him one of the most feared strikers in the Scottish game, and in 1965 he was called up to the Scottish national side to win the first of his 3 caps.

An offer of £50,000 was more than Hibs could afford to refuse, even for their star striker, and so when Sunderland tabled such an offer in October 1965, Martin was on his way to Roker Park. After three years in the North-East, Noel Cantwell brought him to Highfield Road as a replacement for the recently-sold Bobby Gould. He arrived at City in the midst of a relegation battle, with the Sky Blues fighting to preserve their new-found status in the First Division. Martin's 8 goals in 15 games at the end of 1967/68 helped ensure City stayed up. He was forced to miss much of the early part of the following season due to a back injury, and again found himself returning to the side to help them battle against the drop. Once more Martin contributed significantly, netting 9 times – including the last-minute winner against Leicester which finally guaranteed City's survival.

During 1969/70, Martin was prolific, top-scoring with 15 goals, and helping City qualify for their only European campaign to date. His rich vein of form continued into the following year, and he had scored 13 before his surprise departure to Nottingham Forest in February 1971. In his four years at the City Ground, Martin never recaptured his City form, and was hampered by injury troubles. He left in July 1975 for a season with Brighton and then ended his League career with a year at Crystal Palace. After a period in the non-League game with St Patrick's Athletic, Martin moved into coaching, taking up a post in the Middle East. He returned to England in 1981 for a season as part of the management team at Walsall, along with Alan Buckley. In his only season at the helm, the Saddlers finished precariously close to the drop, surviving on goal difference. After leaving Fellows Park he returned for a further spell in the Middle East, before becoming a publican.

	League		FA Cup		League Cup		Other		Total	
	Apps	Goals	Apps	Goals	Apps	Goals	Apps	Goals	Apps	Goals
1967/68	15	8	0	0	0	0	0	0	15	8
1968/69	25	9	2	0	2	0	0	0	29	9
1969/70	40	14	2	1	1	0	0	0	43	15
1970/71	26	9	1	0	5	2	3	2	35	13
TOTAL	106	40	5	1	8	2	3	2	122	45

Dick Mason
Defender, 1946-55

Dick Mason signed for Coventry in 1946, during what was to prove a difficult time for the club in the immediate post-war era. Upon the resumption of League football in time for the 1946/47 season, City fans were expectant, having been raised on the successes of the 1930s. The team still contained many of their favourites from before the war, and the hopes were that they could reproduce the form that had seen City come so close to achieving top-flight status. However, the side was ageing and in decline, and the following seasons would be a time of constant change, as the club tried to recreate the glory days of yesteryear. Mason was to prove to be one of the few constants during this time of turmoil, providing excellent service over eight difficult seasons at Highfield Road.

Mason was twenty-eight when he signed for City, having spent his early career with the Arley Miners' Welfare side, and then with Nuneaton Borough. He made his debut early in the 1946/47 season in the away match at Newcastle, and played his first season as a left half. The following season, he moved to left-back, a position he made his own for the remainder of his time at the club. In his eight seasons with City, Mason missed very few matches, and proved to be a consistent and able performer. By the time he was displaced from the side by Roy Kirk, early in the 1953/54 season, he had made a total of 263 appearances for City.

In February 1955, Mason left Highfield Road to join non-League Bedworth Town, as player-manager. After three seasons, he retired from the game at the age of forty.

	League		FA Cup		Total	
	Apps	Goals	Apps	Goals	Apps	Goals
1946/47	24	0	2	0	26	0
1947/48	36	0	2	0	38	0
1948/49	39	0	1	0	40	0
1949/50	37	0	1	0	38	0
1950/51	36	0	0	0	36	0
1951/52	36	1	1	0	37	1
1952/53	39	1	3	0	42	1
1953/54	6	0	0	0	6	0
TOTAL	253	2	10	0	263	2

George Mason
Centre half, 1931-52

George Mason's status as one of Coventry City's all-time greats is unquestionable. Throughout his twenty-one years at Highfield Road, his professionalism and commitment to the club were never brought into question. His record of 350 appearances, a figure which would have been greatly increased had it not been for the intrusion of the Second World War, ranks him in the top ten of City players in terms of number of games played. Indeed, had it not been for the outbreak of hostilities, it is distinctly possible that Mason may have been the first City player to have earned full international caps for England. As it was, Mason had to make do with two wartime international appearances, which are not recognized in the international records.

Mason was spotted by the then City manager Harry Storer whilst playing for Redhill Amateurs. Recognizing a significant, if raw, talent, Storer signed the eighteen-year-old in November 1931. Over the next three years, Mason learned his trade in the reserve team, his opportunities for first-team football limited by the consistency of Tommy Davidson. Despite making his debut in March 1932, it was not until Davidson was dropped, following an off-the-field disciplinary incident in January 1935, that Mason was able to establish himself as a first-team regular. Within twelve months, Mason was appointed as team captain, succeeding Charlie Bisby, who was also involved with a disciplinary breach and left the club. Throughout the late 1930s, Mason was a lynchpin of the team which won the Third Division (South) championship and then mounted a strong challenge for promotion to the First Division. A number of significant offers for his services were received, each rebuffed by Storer, who placed a great value on defensive strength and stability as the foundation of a successful side.

During the war years, Mason was a regular for City, amassing over 175 wartime appearances. He also guested for Nottingham Forest, during the period when football was suspended in Coventry, following the Blitz. Upon the resumption of peacetime football, Mason continued in the heart of the City defence and remained a key figure in the side for a further three seasons. However, he was now in his mid-thirties and, in October 1949, his place at centre half was taken by Martin McDonnell. Mason remained at the club for a further two years, but only appeared in 8 more games, all in the 1951/52 season. After leaving the club, he spent a short time with non-League Nuneaton Borough, before retiring from the game completely.

	League		FA Cup		Total	
	Apps	Goals	Apps	Goals	Apps	Goals
1931/32	3	0	0	0	3	0
1932/33	6	0	0	0	6	0
1933/34	2	0	0	0	2	0
1934/35	24	0	3	0	27	0
1935/36	40	0	2	0	42	0
1936/37	42	3	3	2	45	5

1937/38	38	1	1	0	39	1
1938/39	42	1	1	0	43	1
1945/46	-	-	2	0	2	0
1946/47	28	0	2	0	30	0
1947/48	34	0	2	0	36	0
1948/49	35	0	1	0	36	0
1949/50	28	1	1	0	29	1
1950/51	0	0	0	0	0	0
1951/52	8	0	2	0	10	0
TOTAL	330	6	20	2	350	8

Reg Matthews
Goalkeeper, 1950-56

Reg Matthews excelled in a struggling City side in the 1950s. His performances earned him the distinction of becoming Coventry's first ever England international, and the first goalkeeper from the Third Division to play at such a level. His agility and consistency was admired throughout the game, and his bravery in goal endeared him to the City faithful who, at the time, had little success to cheer. In many ways, it was inevitable that he would move on to a higher level sooner rather than later, but it was still a big disappointment when he was sold to Chelsea in November 1956, after 116 games for City.

Matthews had signed for Coventry in 1950 from nursery team Modern Machine Tools. However, it was not until three years later, in March 1953, that he was to get his chance in the first team, making his debut in the 0-1 defeat against Southend. Over the next season-and-a-half, he vied with Peter Taylor for the goalie's spot, eventually becoming the regular first-choice 'keeper from September 1954. In his first full season in City's goal, Matthews impressed greatly, earning call-ups to both the England under-23 and 'B' sides, and being selected to represent the Football League. The following season, he progressed on to the full England squad, and made his international debut in the 1-1 draw with Scotland at Hampden Park in April 1956. During his stay at City, he went on to earn 5 England caps – an excellent achievement for someone playing in an average side in the Third Division.

Inevitably, Matthews attracted a great deal of interest from higher division clubs, and with City struggling financially, it was only to be a matter of time before they cashed in on their greatest asset. When Chelsea offered £22,500 in late 1956 – which, at the time, was a world record for a 'keeper – City gratefully accepted and Matthews was on his way to Stamford Bridge. Despite playing at a higher level, Matthews was never again selected for his country, his international career ending with the 1-1 draw against Northern Ireland in October 1956.

In five years with Chelsea, Matthews made 135 appearances, before transferring to Derby County in October 1961. He remained at the Baseball Ground for a further seven years, playing 247 games for the Rams, before retiring from first-class football in 1968. On leaving Derby, Matthews moved into non-League football, taking up the position of player-manager with Rugby Town.

	League		FA Cup		Total	
	Apps	Goals	Apps	Goals	Apps	Goals
1952/53	10	0	0	0	10	0
1953/54	5	0	0	0	5	0
1954/55	36	0	4	0	40	0
1955/56	43	0	1	0	44	0
1956/57	17	0	0	0	17	0
TOTAL	111	0	5	0	116	0

Reg Matthews in action for City.

Frank Mobley

Forward, 1890-92 and 1900-01

Frank Mobley joined Singers FC in 1890, at a time when the team were known as 'The Little Blackbirds' due to their relative size, and the fact that they wore black and red shirts. He became a legend with the Singers faithful, and soon established himself as one of the foremost centre-forwards of the 1890s, linking up in a dynamic forward line with early heroes Harry Banks and Will Dorrell. In his first season with the club he scored in excess of twenty goals including the winner in the Birmingham Cup final, in which Singers beat Willenhall Pickwicks 1-0 at Aston Villa's Perry Bar Ground. His second season was one of further success for Singers, with the club achieving a unique cup treble. In addition to the Birmingham & District Junior Cup which they successfully defended, the little Blackbirds were also triumphant in he Walsall Cup and the Wednesbury Cup. In cup-ties alone that season, Mobley scored a mammoth 26 goals, including 16 in just 3 consecutive matches; the 12-1 win over Small Heath (five goals), the 11-0 victory over Burlington EMS (five goals) and the 12-2 rout of Soho Villa (six goals).

Mobley's goalscoring feats inevitably attracted the attention of 'bigger' clubs of the time, and in the close season of 1892/93 he signed for Small Heath along with Harry Edwards. He remained with the Birmingham club for four years, playing 103 games and scoring 64 goals before moving to Bury in May 1896. His stay with the Shakers was brief and he made only three appearances in October of the same year, before transferring to Gravesend in the Southern League. After a spell with Warmley in Bristol, he returned to Highfield Road for a season in 1900/1901.

Mobley's 'farewell' season saw City struggle in the Birmingham and District League and suffer some disastrous defeats. Mobley made 21 appearances during the campaign, and scored seven, however, his skills did little to lift the side who were greatly outclassed by many of their rivals. In all the team conceded 101 goals over the course of the season's 34 matches, including five or more on no fewer than eight occasions. Mobley faced the ignominy of being part of the team which suffered the heaviest defeat in all competitions in the twentieth century, when Coventry lost 14-1 to Aston Villa Reserves in December 1900. It was a less than fitting end to his association with Coventry, and one could have forgiven a degree of relief when he finally retired at the end of the campaign. After his retirement he moved to Birmingham where he set up a business. He died in 1940, aged seventy-two.

	League		FA Cup		Total	
	Apps	Goals	Apps	Goals	Apps	Goals
1900/01	21	7	0	0	21	7
TOTAL	21	7	0	0	21	7

Bill Morgan
Goalkeeper, 1932-44

In terms of goalkeeping, Coventry have been blessed with excellence in abundance over the years. From Nat Robinson and Bob Evans in the pre-League era, through to Steve Ogrizovic and Magnus Hedman in recent years, there has been a steady flow of quality 'keepers protecting the City net. Bill Morgan was no exception, proving to be an outstanding custodian in the heady years of the late 1930s. Behind the consistent defensive line of Astley, Metcalf, Frith and Mason, he provided a sturdy final barrier in a City team striving for promotion to the First Division. Morgan was yet another player whose career was brought to an end due to the war, playing his final League game at the age of only twenty-five.

Newcastle-born Morgan was playing for the Mickley Colliery side, when Harry Storer was alerted to his talents. He noticed the seventeen-year-old in an excellent FA Cup performance against Blyth Spartans in 1931, and signed him for Coventry immediately. His debut came a year later in the 1-0 defeat against Brighton, one of 8 games he played during 1932/33. For the next three seasons, Morgan remained as understudy to first-choice 'keeper, Horace Pearson, getting only limited opportunities in the first team. In early 1936, Pearson was dropped, after a number of disappointing performances, and Morgan got his

chance in the first team. He never looked back, missing only two games between then and the war, during which time he kept 51 clean sheets.

He continued to play for the wartime side, and also guested for both Nottingham Forest and Leicester City, during the suspension of football in Coventry between the Blitz and the start of the 1942/43 season. It was during a match for Leicester, that Morgan sustained an shoulder injury, which would eventually bring his career to an end. He continued to play until early 1944, but was suffering from increasing discomfort in his shoulder. In February 1944, he finally took medical advice and retired from the game. A brief coaching career with City's nursery side, Modern Machines, followed, before he left the game completely in 1953.

| | League | | FA Cup | | Total | |
	Apps	Goals	Apps	Goals	Apps	Goals
1932/33	8	0	0	0	8	0
1933/34	4	0	0	0	4	0
1934/35	2	0	1	0	3	0
1935/36	12	0	0	0	12	0
1936/37	42	0	3	0	45	0
1937/38	41	0	1	0	42	0
1938/39	41	0	1	0	42	0
TOTAL	150	0	6	0	156	0

Dennis Mortimer
Midfield, 1969-75

Dennis Mortimer was a product of the highly successful youth programme at Highfield Road in the late 1960s, and was captain of the 1970 Youth Cup final team, who lost a marathon battle with Spurs after a second replay. Of the seven members of that team who would graduate to first-team football for City, Mortimer was arguably the most naturally gifted and technically adept. He possessed excellent close skill, and exuded a natural confidence, which made him a real favourite with the fans.

Mortimer made his City debut in October 1969, appearing as a substitute against West Ham whilst still only seventeen. He impressed in early appearances, and by midway through the following season, he had won a regular first-team place in the City midfield. Thus began six seasons of regular football at Highfield Road, during which time Mortimer developed into an outstanding player, more than fulfilling his early promise. By 1972, Mortimer was attracting the attention of the international selectors, making his England under-23 debut against Wales. He won 6 caps at this level during his time at City, and would go on to represent the England 'B' team after leaving Highfield Road. However, the full international call-up would always evade him.

In December 1975, the shock announcement was made that Mortimer had been sold to Aston Villa for £175,000. His premature departure from Highfield Road caused an outcry amongst fans, who accused the club of lacking ambition. The reality was that the books needed to be balanced after the £240,000 purchase of Larry Lloyd. Once Willie Carr's proposed move to Wolves had broken down, Mortimer was the Sky Blues' most saleable asset, who could generate the necessary funds. It is a cruel irony that, while Mortimer's career flourished during the Villa glory years, Lloyd proved to be a costly flop at City.

Mortimer spent a highly successful ten years at Villa Park, winning the League Cup in 1977, and captaining the side to the League Championship and European Cup in the early 1980s. He left Villa in 1985, spending a year on the South Coast with Brighton, before ending his League career with Birmingham City. From the Blues, he dropped into non-League football, first with Kettering Town, and, in 1988, he became player-manager at Redditch United.

	League Apps	Goals	FA Cup Apps	Goals	League Cup Apps	Goals	Other Apps	Goals	Total Apps	Goals
1969/70	6 (3)	0	1	0	0	0	0	0	7 (3)	0
1970/71	24 (3)	0	0	0	2	0	1	0	27 (3)	0
1971/72	26 (8)	4	1 (1)	0	1	0	2 (1)	1	30 (10)	5
1972/73	39	1	4	0	2	0	2	1	47	2
1973/74	33	1	3	0	3	0	2	0	41	1
1974/75	29	3	0	0	1	0	0	0	30	3
1975/76	22	1	0	0	2	0	0	0	24	1
TOTAL	179 (14)	10	9 (1)	0	11	0	7 (1)	2	206 (16)	12

Peter Murphy
Inside left, 1943-50

Had it not been for the outbreak of the Second World War, Peter Murphy could well have become a Middlesborough player and plied his footballing trade in his native North-East. Just on the day before war was declared, Murphy had a trial with Boro's nursery side, Southbank St Peter's, and had impressed enough to earn the promise of a recall – however, in the confusion that followed, the recall never came. He moved to the Midlands during the war and began playing amateur football with the Dunlop team in Birmingham. It was whilst playing for Dunlop, that he was spotted by Coventry and brought to Highfield Road. A period in the armed forces delayed his debut, and meant that it wasn't until midway through the 1946/47 season that he was able to commence his football career in earnest.

Murphy made his City debut in December 1946 as inside left in the 1-0 win over Fulham. It was one of just 12 appearances during the first post-war campaign, and it wasn't until the following season that he was able to establish himself as a regular in the first team. He quickly developed into an effective left-sided playmaker, who was equally able to turn goalscorer, as well as create opportunities for others. During 1948/49, he established a prolific partnership with Ted Roberts, contributing 13 of the pair's 32 goals. The following year, it was Murphy's turn to head the scoring chart, netting 15 in what was to be his final campaign as a City player.

Inevitably, Murphy's performances had been attracting the attention of First Division clubs, and in the close season of 1950, Tottenham offered £18,500 for the inside forward. City's finances were such that they could ill-afford to refuse such a bid, and Murphy duly became a Spurs player, after 120 appearances and 37 goals for the Bantams. In his first season at White Hart Lane, he was part of the side that won the League Championship. However, he found himself unable to settle in London, and after only two years, he moved back to the Midlands to join Birmingham City for £20,000.

Murphy's time at St Andrews was the most settled and productive of his career, and he spent eight successful years with the Blues. His scoring record during his stay amounted to almost a goal every other game, as he helped the side to the Second Division championship in 1955 and the FA Cup final a year later. Murphy emerged from his only Wembley final with a runners-up medal, after Birmingham were defeated 3-1 by Manchester City, and he was involved in the unfortunate incident which resulted in the Manchester 'keeper, Bert Trautmann, breaking his neck. After eight years and over 250 appearances for the Blues, Murphy retired from League football at the age of thirty-eight. He spent a further year in the non-League game with Rugby Town, before retiring completely.

	League		FA Cup		Total	
	Apps	Goals	Apps	Goals	Apps	Goals
1946/47	11	2	1	0	12	2
1947/48	29	7	2	0	31	7
1948/49	36	13	1	0	37	13
1949/50	39	15	1	0	40	15
TOTAL	115	37	5	0	120	37

Peter Ndlovu
Forward, 1991-97

It was on the tour of Zimbabwe in the summer of 1990, that John Sillett spotted the raw talent of Peter Ndlovu, who was playing for local team Bulawayo Highlanders. Ndlovu was only seventeen at the time, but was already an established Zimbabwean international, having made his debut for the national team when only fifteen. Sillett invited Ndlovu, along with his brother, Adam, to Coventry for a trial, and he was signed on as a professional by Terry Butcher a year later. Butcher had originally wanted to sign both brothers, but a work permit could only be obtained for one, and Peter was his choice. The fee payable to Highlanders of Zimbabwe was a bargain £10,000 – small change in modern British football, but a significant sum to the Africans.

Ndlovu made his full debut against Everton in September 1991, and was gradually introduced into the side. His great pace and excellent close ball control made him a wonderfully exciting player to watch, and, although somewhat erratic at times, he delighted the Highfield Road crowd with displays of exceptional skill. Some of Ndlovu's goals for City were a true delight, and although he would often frustrate with missed opportunities, he scored some of the most memorable goals of the 1990s whilst at Highfield Road. In his first season at City, he played in 26 games, 15 as substitute, but became a first-team regular in 1992/93. By the summer of 1993, Ndlovu was attracting the attention of some of England's top clubs, and transfer speculation was rife, with fees in excess of £3 million being touted. It was the possibility of Ndlovu being sold, which Bobby Gould cited as a major reason for his resignation in October 1993. However the sale never came, and Ndlovu continued as a City player. In 1994/95, he amassed 13 goals for City, including a stunning hat-trick against Liverpool, and he began to form a good understanding with newly signed Dion Dublin. His international commitments reduced his appearances for City, but the regular travelling did little to dampen his on-field displays. In 1995/96, he became Coventry's most capped player, overtaking the long-standing record shared by Dave Clememts and Ronnie Rees. He went on to appear 26 times for his country whilst at Highfield Road. In the summer of 1996, Ndlovu was struck by a serious knee injury, picked up while on duty for Zimbabwe. He required two operations on the damaged knee, but it continued to be a source of niggling trouble for the player. A year later, he was allowed to join Birmingham City, the fee being negotiated on a pay-as-you-play basis, because of worries over his fitness. Ndlovu remained at St Andrews for three years, before being loaned out to Huddersfield Town in December 2000, and then signing for Sheffield United in 2001.

	League		FA Cup		League Cup		Other		Total	
	Apps	Goals	Apps	Goals	Apps	Goals	Apps	Goals	Apps	Goals
1991/92	9(14)	2	0	0	2	0	0(1)	0	11(15)	2
1992/93	27 (5)	7	1	0	1	0	0	0	29 (5)	7
1993/94	40	11	1	0	2	0	0	0	43	11
1994/95	28 (2)	11	3	2	1	0	0	0	32 (2)	13
1995/96	27 (5)	5	0(1)	0	4	1	0	0	31 (5)	6
1996/97	10(10)	1	0(3)	0	0	0	0	0	10(13)	1
TOTAL	141(36)	37	5(4)	2	10	1	0(1)	0	156(40)	40

Roland Nilsson

Right-back, 1997-99 & 2001- present; manager 2001-present

In his first spell at Highfield Road, Roland Nilsson became known simply as 'The Legend', such was the regard in which he was held by both fans and team-mates alike. A model professional, Nilsson was a stylish and accomplished right-back who rarely had an off-day at Highfield Road. He was a worthy successor to Brian Borrows who had left the season before Nilsson's arrival, and he is considered by many to be one of the finest players to have ever pulled on a Sky Blue shirt. His return to City after an absence of two years was greeted with universal delight, and his unforeseen elevation to manager in September 2001 heralded a new era at Highfield Road.

By the time of his arrival at Highfield Road in 1997, Nilsson had already established a formidable reputation on both the domestic and international circuits. He began playing in his native Sweden with IFK Gothenburg, where he began his long and distinguished international career, and he also enjoyed European success in the UEFA Cup in 1987. Ron Atkinson brought him to England in 1989 to join Sheffield Wednesday for a fee of £375,000. Again, he enjoyed success at Wednesday, and despite being relegated in his first season, the club were promoted the following year winning the League Cup along the way. In 1990 he played in both domestic cup finals, as Wednesday were beaten each time by Arsenal.

After five years and 186 appearances at Hillsborough, Nilsson returned to Sweden to play for his hometown club of Hellsingborgs, spending three years back on home soil before Atkinson tempted him to return to England with the Sky Blues. His debut for City saw the daunting task of marking Ryan Giggs at Old Trafford, a job he resolutely undertook, despite City losing 3-0. Nilsson became an instant regular in the first team, impressing not only with his obvious talent, but with his exceptional fitness for a player in his mid-thirties. He also reached the milestone of 100 international appearances during his first season with City, a figure unsurpassed in Swedish history.

1998/99 proved to be Nilsson's last, before announcing his retirement and returning again to Sweden. He played in 29 matches in his final season, maintaining the performance level that had seen him so welcomed in his first campaign. Once back in Scandinavia, he took up the position of director of football at Helsingborgs, a post which had been especially created for him.

Nilsson returned to Highfield Road in the summer of 2001 to take up a player/coach position under Gordon Strachan. Upon Strachan's departure in September 2001, Nilsson was asked to take on the manager's role, initially as a caretaker. His appointment spurred an immediate turnaround in the team's fortunes, and after six wins and one draw in his first eight games in charge, his appointment was made permanent in October 2001.

	League		FA Cup		League Cup			Total	
	Apps	Goals	Apps	Goals	Apps	Goals		Apps	Goals
1997/98	32	0	4	0	3	0		39	0
1998/99	27	0	2	0	0	0		29	0
2001/02(up to 26/11/01)	8	0	0	0	1	0		9	0
TOTAL	67	0	6	0	3	0		77	0

Steve Ogrizovic
Goalkeeper, 1984-2000

The name of Steve Ogrizovic will forever be synonymous with the Sky Blues of the 1980s and '90s. In an era when the club loyalty of players was regularly brought into question, Oggy's career at City spanned sixteen years over three decades, before he finally bowed out of the first team in May 2000. Ogrizovic began his career at Chesterfield in 1977, near to his hometown of Mansfield. He played a mere 16 games for the Derbyshire club, before being signed by Bob Paisley at Liverpool, as cover for Ray Clemence. Clemence's dominance at Anfield limited Ogrizovic's chances at Liverpool, as did the arrival of Bruce Grobelaar, when Clemence left for Spurs. Ogrizovic made only 4 appearances in five years for the Reds, before joining Shrewsbury Town in 1982. He spent two years at Gay Meadow, and then signed for City in a move worth £72,500.

Ogrizovic started his City career in the best possible manner, with his debut in the opening match of the 1984/85 season commencing a consecutive run of 209 League games (equalling Alf Wood's club record). If one includes cup matches, his tally of consecutive games reached an unmatched 241. As well as winning the FA Cup during this period, Ogrizovic also became the first City 'keeper to score a League goal, beating the unfortunate Martin Hodge of Sheffield Wednesday in October 1986. In Oggy's own words: 'I think I was about six to eight yards from my own goal line, when I kicked it out of my hands. I was trying to kick long for Cyrille Regis and Dave Bennett to run on to, but Cyrille gave up the chase because the wind took it. It bounced on the edge of the penalty area, over Martin Hodge and was deflected into the net off the post.' His run was eventually brought to an end in March 1989, when he was injured during the match against Millwall and forced to miss the following week's fixture versus Luton.

Until breaking his leg in 1995, Ogrizovic missed only a handful of matches for City. At the time of his injury, he was nearing thirty-eight, and for most players this would have signalled an end to their career. However, Ogrizovic battled his way back to fitness and regained the number one jersey just seven months later. He remained a regular in the side until 1998, before finally being superceded in the City goal by Magnus Hedman. Oggy remained as understudy to Hedman for a further two years, passing the landmark of 600 games for the club in the 1999/2000 season. After sixteen years at City, he announced his retirement at the end of the season, and made an emotional farewell in the final game against Sheffield Wednesday. A grateful crowd gave him a standing ovation after the match, as Oggy took a deserved lap of honour. Perhaps the only negative in his time at City was the lack of international honours that many felt he deserved. As with many City players, he was overlooked by successive England managers, when he was in the prime of form and matched any in the international frame. His only representative honour was a seventeen-minute appearance as a second-half substitute for the Football League in the Centenary match against the Rest of the World in 1987.

	League		FA Cup		League Cup		Other		Total	
	Apps	Goals	Apps	Goals	Apps	Goals	Apps	Goals	Apps	Goals
1984/85	42	0	2	0	2	0	0	0	46	0
1985/86	42	0	1	0	4	0	2	0	49	0
1986/87	42	1	6	0	5	0	1	0	54	1
1987/88	40	0	2	0	3	0	4	0	49	0
1988/89	38	0	1	0	3	0	1	0	43	0
1989/90	37	0	1	0	7	0	1	0	46	0
1990/91	37	0	4	0	5	0	1	0	47	0
1991/92	38	0	2	0	3	0	1	0	44	0
1992/93	33	0	1	0	2	0	0	0	36	0
1993/94	33	0	1	0	3	0	0	0	37	0
1994/95	33	0	4	0	3	0	0	0	40	0
1995/96	25	0	3	0	1	0	0	0	29	0
1996/97	38	0	4	0	4	0	0	0	46	0
1997/98	24	0	2	0	4	0	0	0	30	0
1998/99	2	0	0	0	0	0	0	0	2	0
1999/2000	3	0	0	0	0	0	0	0	3	0
TOTAL	507	1	34	0	49	0	11	0	601	1

Harry Parkes
Outside right, 1908-14

Harry Parkes's long career in football began with local Birmingham sides, Coombs Wood and Halesowen, before joining West Bromwich as an seventeen-year-old in February 1906. Parkes spent two years at the Hawthorns, appearing in their FA Cup semi-final in 1907, whilst still only seventeen. He signed for Coventry in 1908, following a dispute with Albion over terms, and made his debut in the Christmas Day draw with Swindon.

Parkes was an exciting right-winger, full of pace and ever able to deliver the cross to his colleagues in the centre. His appearances in his first two years at Highfield Road were restricted, due to the consistency of Charlie Tickle in the outside right position. However, in time for the 1910/11 season, Tickle reverted to inside right, allowing Parkes to establish himself on City's right flank. He quickly became a favourite at City, and thrived in the exciting Southern League side of the early 1910s. In 1910/11, he was top scorer for the club with 12 goals, a feat he bettered in 1912/13, this time with 13. It was as a provider, however, that he was best known, his crosses creating many goalscoring opportunities.

After six seasons with Coventry, Parkes returned to West Brom at the end of the 1913/14 season. In his five seasons back with the Throstles, he combined his playing role with that of assistant manager, beginning what would be a long career in the management side of the game. He moved to Newport County in 1919 as secretary-manager, and played his last games while at Somerton Park. His managerial career saw him take charge of Chesterfield (1922-27), Lincoln City (1927-36), Mansfield Town (1936-38), and Notts County (1938-39). Highlights during his twenty years in management included presiding over Newport's inaugural League season in 1921/22, and winning the Third Division (North) championship in 1931/32 with Lincoln City. He retired from the game after leaving Notts County, and lived in Nottingham until his death in 1948.

| | Southern League | | FA Cup | | | Total | |
	Apps	Goals	Apps	Goals		Apps	Goals
1908/09	11	2	0	0		11	2
1909/10	11	1	0	0		11	1
1910/11	33	11	4	1		37	12
1911/12	36	7	2	1		38	8
1912/13	38	12	2	1		40	13
1913/14	32	2	1	0		33	2
TOTAL	161	35	9	3		170	38

Trevor Peake

Centre half, 1983-91

Born in Nuneaton, Peake began his playing career with non-League Nuneaton Borough, with whom he remained until the age of twenty-two. He excelled there, representing England at semi-professional level, before making the step-up into League football with Lincoln City. At Sincil Bank, he rapidly gained a reputation as an accomplished central defender, possessing a classy touch and an excellent sense of timing. He remained with the Imps for four years, before becoming one of Bobby Gould's first signings for Coventry in the summer of 1983. The fee, a mere £100,000, was to prove money well spent, as Peake went on to serve City consistently over the next nine seasons.

He made his debut for City in the away match against Spurs in August 1983. During his opening season with the club, he partnered Sam Allardyce in the heart of City's defence, playing a total of 40 matches. However, in the close season of 1984, Allardyce left and, as his replacement, Gould signed Notts County defender Brian Kilcline. Thus began one of the most consistent central defensive partnerships of recent years, with Peake and Kilcline marshalling City's defence successfully for the next seven seasons. In his first season with the club, Peake was club captain, a position he lost following a disagreement with Don MacKay. Despite this setback, he continued as a regular in the team throughout his City career, the highlight, of course, coming with the cup success in 1987. In 1987/88, he was selected for the England 'B' squad, but was unable to play, due to injury. This was to be his only professional call-up at international level, a fact which many Coventry fans view as a travesty.

Upon the arrival of Terry Butcher as player-manager in 1990, Peake's playing days at City were numbered, with Butcher looking to dispense with the old guard and build a team for the future. Peake's City career, however, ended on a sour note, being transfer-listed following an off-field incident on the pre-season tour of Scotland in 1991. This resulted in a transfer to Luton Town in August of the same year, when Peake would have clearly been happy to have remained at Highfield Road. It was an unfortunate end to a great City career, and many fans felt deeply unhappy with the way Butcher had treated a great servant of the club.

By the time he left, Peake had made 334 appearances for City, a record which places him tenth in the all-time appearances list for the club. He went on to play a further 202 games for Luton, amassing a total of well over 500 appearances in his League career. Peake returned to City once his playing days were over, taking up a position on the coaching staff. He remains at the club, and is currently manager of the reserve side.

	League		FA Cup		League Cup		Other		Total	
	Apps	Goals	Apps	Goals	Apps	Goals	Apps	Goals	Apps	Goals
1983/84	33	3	4	1	3	0	0	0	40	4
1984/85	33(1)	1	1	0	2	0	0	0	36 (1)	1
1985/86	37	1	1	0	4	0	2	0	44	1
1986/87	39	0	6	0	4	0	1	0	50	0
1987/88	31	0	1	0	2	0	4	0	38	0
1988/89	32	0	1	0	2	0	1	0	36	0
1989/90	33	0	1	0	8	0	1	0	43	0
1990/91	36	1	2	0	5	0	1	0	44	1
1991/92	2	0	0	0	0	0	0	0	2	0
TOTAL	276(1)	6	17	1	30	0	10	0	333 (1)	7

Barry Powell
Midfield, 1975-79

Born in Kenilworth, Barry Powell was the son of former Wales and Aston Villa wing-half, Ivor Powell. He began his career with Wolves, signing for the Molineux club in January 1972 at the age of eighteen. He spent four years at Molineux, establishing himself as a regular in the Wolves midfield during the 1973/74 season. In the spring of 1974, he featured in the side which beat Manchester City at Wembley to lift the League Cup, and also made his debut for the England under-23 side, one of 5 caps he would win at this level. However, by 1975, Powell found himself wanting for regular first-team football with Wolves, and, after a spell on loan in with American Portland Timbers, he was signed by Gordon Milne for City in September 1975, in a deal worth £75,000.

Powell made his debut in September 1975 in the 3-1 cup win over Bolton, and slotted effortlessly into the midfield throughout 1975/76, initially alongside Denis Mortimer. The following year saw the arrival of Terry Yorath from Leeds, and Powell quickly formed an excellent central partnership with the Welsh captain. Powell's creative play complemented Yorath's robust and tough-tackling style, and the combination proved very effective throughout the late 1970s. The pairing was at its best through the successful 1977/78 season, in which Powell was ever present and helped City to a seventh-place finish in the First Division. In 1978/79, Powell took on the responsibility of regular penalty taker, scoring 8 of his 29 goals for City from the spot.

Within the space of a month, in late 1979, both Powell and Yorath were sold by City, both citing a desire for greater success as part of their reasons for moving. Of equal importance in the decision was City's need for finance, with Powell's sale to Derby raising £350,000. Powell spent two years at the Baseball Ground, the second of which was in the Second Division, after Derby's relegation in 1980. After another summer in Portland, USA, he linked up with Tommy Hutchison for the Hong Kong side, Bulova, in August 1982, returning to England in 1984 – again to play alongside Hutchison, first at Burnley and then Swansea City. Another brief spell in Hong Kong followed, before Powell finished his career with two years at Wolves up until 1988.

	League		FA Cup		League Cup		Total	
	Apps	Goals	Apps	Goals	Apps	Goals	Apps	Goals
1975/76	32(2)	7	1(1)	0	1	0	34 (3)	7
1976/77	40	4	2	0	1	0	43	4
1977/78	42	3	1	0	4	2	47	5
1978/79	38	9	2	0	1	0	41	9
1979/80	10	4	0	0	2	0	12	4
TOTAL	162(2)	27	6(1)	0	9	2	177 (3)	29

Mickey Quinn
Centre forward, 1992-95

Mickey Quinn was one of the more unlikely goalscoring heroes of recent years. In an era when professional footballers are expected to be superfit models of athleticism, with the body perfect, Quinn's less-than-lithe figure attracted more than a passing comment, and a barrage of light-hearted ribbing from the fans. Whatever his physique, Quinn proved more than able to score a hatful of goals wherever he played, and, although he would never win any prizes for the 100 metres, in his own words he was 'faster than anyone over two yards in the box'.

By the time he arrived at Highfield Road, Quinn was a seasoned professional of five clubs standing. He had begun his career with Wigan in the late 1970s, but left without playing a game to join Stockport five years later. After 70 games and 41 goals for Stockport, he made the short move to Boundary Park, where he continued to score freely for two seasons. From Lancashire, Quinn travelled south to Portsmouth, where his goals saw the club make a brief sojourn to the top flight in 1986. Three years at Fratton Park were followed by three further seasons at St James' for Newcastle United, following in the striking tradition of such names as Hughie Gallacher and Malcolm McDonald.

It was from Newcastle that Bobby Gould brought Quinn to Coventry, initially as a loanee, in November 1992. Quinn's impact at Highfield Road was immediate, scoring 10 times in the first 6 games, to ensure that the loan deal was made a permanent transfer. He ended the season as top scorer with 17 goals, despite missing the first 15 games of the campaign. 1993/94 started as Quinn had left off in the previous year, with a blistering hat-trick in City's 3-0 win at Highbury on the opening day. Inexplicably, however, the goals began to dry up at this point, and lean spells, unprecedented in his career, resulted in Quinn notching just 9 in 35 matches. The end of Quinn's brief stay at Highfield Road was signalled early in the following season, when he was dropped just three games into the campaign. He made a further three appearances as a substitute, but failed to score, and later in the year was loaned out to both Plymouth and Watford. Quinn finally left in July 1995, to join Greek side PAOK Salonika, but his stay was brief, making only 10 appearances before returning to England and leaving the game.

After retiring as a player, Quinn embarked on a career in his other favoured sporting pastime of horse racing. Under the tutelage of fellow ex-professional, Mick Channon, Quinn learned the ropes and became a qualified trainer of racehorses, until being suspended in 2001.

	League		FA Cup		League Cup		Total	
	Apps	Goals	Apps	Goals	Apps	Goals	Apps	Goals
1992/93	26	17	1	0	0	0	27	17
1993/94	28(4)	8	0(1)	0	1(1)	1	29 (6)	9
1994/95	3(3)	0	0	0	0	0	3 (3)	0
TOTAL	57(7)	25	1(1)	0	1(1)	1	59 (9)	28

John (Jackie) Randall
Full-back, 1922-27

During the turbulent 1920s, Jackie Randle provided a much needed mainstay in the City team, his solid defensive displays making him a first-team regular over five seasons at Highfield Road. Equally at home on either the left or right side of defence, Randle was a tough-tackling, no-nonsense player, who was renowned for the power of his clearances. At a time when the turnover of players was high, Randle provided consistency in the team, as it strove to consolidate its new-found status in the League.

Born in Bedworth, he began his career with Exhall Colliery, where he combined his football with working down the mine. It was whilst playing for Exhall, that Randle was spotted by City manager Albert Evans, who brought him to Highfield Road in the latter part of the 1921/22 season. He remained in the reserves for two seasons, before getting his opportunity in the first team at the start of 1923/24. He quickly impressed with consistently excellent displays, and played 40 games as City struggled to maintain their place in the Second Division.

Over the course of five seasons, Randle made 156 appearances for City, including being ever present in 1925/26. His most famous game in City colours, however, was memorable for all the wrong reasons. In the League match against Bristol City in September 1926, Randle earned the unenviable record of being the only City player to have scored a hat-trick of own goals in a game. Ironically, it was the only time that Randle's name ever appeared on the scoresheet during a Coventry match.

After five years at City, Randle transferred to Birmingham in November 1927, for what was then a club record fee of £1,000. During his time at the Blues, he played regularly in the First Division, but suffered the disappointment of missing the FA Cup final in 1931, in which Birmingham lost 2-1 to West Brom. In his six years at St Andrews, he went on to make 116 appearances, before switching to Bournmouth and Boscombe Athletic in 1933. After a year on the South Coast, Randle moved on, first to Guildford City and then to Newdigate, where he ended his playing career.

	League		FA Cup		Total	
	Apps	Goals	Apps	Goals	Apps	Goals
1923/24	38	0	2	0	40	0
1924/25	28	0	1	0	29	0
1925/26	42	0	1	0	43	0
1926/27	29	0	3	0	32	0
1927/28	12	0	0	0	12	0
TOTAL	149	0	7	0	156	0

Ronnie Rees
Winger, 1962-68

Jimmy Hill's first full season as Coventry City's manager was a mere nine games old when he launched the career of an eighteen-year-old former youth team player called Ronnie Rees. The outside-left position in Hill's new forward line was proving a difficulty, with new-signing Bobby Laverick not making the grade. Consequently, Hill thrust Rees into first-team action, by his own admission, sooner than he would have wished. He did not disappoint however, and immediately made the left flank his own. It was the start of what would be six years of excellent service to City, during which Rees' attacking prowess contributed significantly to Coventry's rise to the First Division.

Born in Ystradgynlais on 4 April 1944, Rees joined Coventry as an apprentice at the turn of the 1960s. He signed professional forms with the club in May 1962, four months before his impromptu debut in the September of the same year. His first game was in the home match against Shrewsbury, which ended in a goalless draw, and he went on to make 42 appearances during the 1962/63 campaign, scoring 5 goals. Rees also won his first international honours during the same season, a call up to the Wales under-23 side for the game against Scotland being the first of 7 caps he would win at this level.

During the promotion winning season of 1963/64, Rees was an ever-present, his consistently excellent service to front men George Hudson and Ken Hale giving City a dynamic attacking thrust. He also proved himself far from goal-shy with 15 strikes, his best tally for any single season with the Sky Blues. A particular highlight came in the October victory over Shrewsbury, in which Rees registered his first hat-trick as City romped to an 8-1 victory. It was only a matter of time before a full Welsh international call-up came, and in October 1964, Rees won his first full cap for his country. His debut came in the 3-2 win over Scotland in Cardiff, in a Welsh side which included greats such as John Charles, Ivor Allchurch and Cliff Jones. Rees proved eminently able in such illustrious company, and became a regular on the Welsh flank, winning 21 caps during his time at Highfield Road, and 39 in total.

Rees played a fundamental role in the side throughout Coventry's three seasons in the Second Division, missing only six games. His ability to play on either flank was demonstrated in long spells on the right, and offered an extra dynamic to the side as it pushed for top-flight status. He missed only three games in the promotion campaign of 1966/67, scoring 5 goals, including one in the championship decider against Wolves. His First Division career at Coventry, however, proved short lived. Midway through the 1967/68 campaign, with City struggling against relegation, manager Noel Cantwell was forced to make sacrifices to balance the books following the purchases of Ernie Hunt, Neil Martin and Chris Cattlin. Rees was a saleable asset, and a fee of £65,000 saw him move across the Midlands to join West Bromwich Albion in March 1968. In all he had made 262 appearances for City, scoring 52 goals.

Rees remained at the Hawthorns for just over a year, before joining Nottingham Forest in a £60,0000 move in February 1969. After three years with Forest he returned to Wales to join Swansea City in January 1972. He saw out his playing career at the Vetch Field, finally retiring as a player at the end of 1974/75, at the relatively young age of thirty-one.

	League		FA Cup		League Cup		Total	
	Apps	Goals	Apps	Goals	Apps	Goals	Apps	Goals
1962/63	33	4	8	0	1	1	42	5
1963/64	46	13	2	1	2	1	50	15
1964/65	41	7	1	0	4	2	46	9
1965/66	41	7	3	2	4	0	48	9
1966/67	39	3	1	1	3	1	43	5
1967/68	30	8	2	1	1	0	33	9
TOTAL	230	42	17	5	15	5	262	52

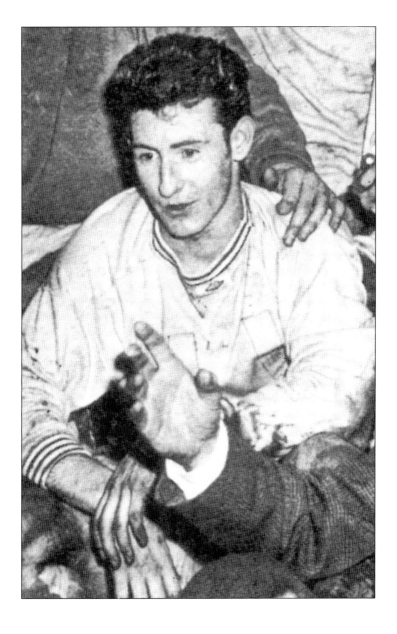

Cyrille Regis
Centre forward, 1984-91

Born in Maripiasoula in French Guyana on 9 February 1958, Regis was spotted whilst playing for non-League Hayes, by the then chief scout for the Baggies, Ronnie Allen. On Allen's recommendation, he was signed in May 1977 for a fee of £5,000. He quickly became a crucial part of Ron Atkinson's exciting West Brom team that were never far away from the top of the First Division. Regis top scored for the Baggies on three occasions and his performances at the Hawthorns earned him international call-ups at both Under-21 and 'B' levels, before a full debut for England in the 4-0 win over Northern Ireland in February 1982. Widely tipped for inclusion in Ron Greenwood's squad for the World Cup finals in Spain, Regis unfortunately picked up a late injury which put paid to his chances. He eventually made 4 full international appearances whilst at West Brom, a total which many speculate could have been much higher had he of played for a more 'fashionable' club.

After 237 League games, and 82 goals for West Brom, Regis was became one of Bobby Gould's last signings for the Sky Blues when he came to Highfield Road for £300,000 in October 1984. Competition for Regis' signature was stiff, and Gould had to vie with (most noticably) Manchester United to land his man. Regis' Highfield Road career got off to a slow start, with criticism being levelled at his low strike rate, particularly in his first two seasons. His debut campaign in 1984/85 saw Regis net only 5 times in 32 appearances, with the figure doubled in 1985/86. He did, however, play a crucial role in maintaining City's top-flight status in his first season at the club, scoring two in the last-day relegation battle with Champions Everton.

It was not until the Sillett and Curtis era that Coventry saw the best of Regis, and he became a firm favourite with the Highfield Road faithful. City's free-flowing attacking style under Sillett was well suited to Regis, and he formed a successful understanding with an equally rejuvenated Dave Bennett. His role in the 1987 Cup-winning run will long be remembered as will the disappointment he suffered when netting in the final only for the goal to be disallowed. Regis' return to form earned him a recall to the England squad, and four months after the Cup Final success, he earned his fifth and final cap with a substitute appearance versus Turkey.

Whilst never prolific at Highfield Road, his total of 62 goals for City ranks him eleventh in the overall goalscoring charts and second in the top-flight era to Dion Dublin. His highest tally in a single match came in the 7-2 League Cup win over Chester City in 1985, a total which still remains a record for the club in this competition.

	League		FA Cup		League Cup		Other		Total	
	Apps	Goals	Apps	Goals	Apps	Goals	Apps	Goals	Apps	Goals
1984/85	30(1)	5	1	0	0	0	0	0	31 (1)	5
1985/86	34	5	1	0	2	5	0	0	37	10
1986/87	40	12	6	2	5	2	0	0	51	16
1987/88	30(1)	10	2	1	2	1	2	0	36 (1)	12
1988/89	34	7	1	0	3	0	0	0	38	7
1989/90	32(2)	4	0(1)	0	7	1	1	0	40 (3)	5
1990/91	31(3)	4	4	0	5	3	1	0	41 (3)	7
TOTAL	231(7)	47	15(1)	3	24	12	4	0	274 (8)	62

Brian 'Harry' Roberts
Defender, 1974-84

While Brian Roberts could never have been described as the most cultured of players, he was, nevertheless, a solid and dependable player for City over the course of nine seasons. 'Harry', as he was known, was a great favourite with the fans and one of the game's characters, enlivening what were dark days in the early 1980s. After joining the club as an apprentice, he signed professional forms in May 1974, although he would not make his debut for a further two years. In the interim, experience was gained during a loan spell at John Sillett's Hereford United, in early 1975. His debut came in April 1976, in a match where Coventry were soundly beaten 4-1 by Tottenham.

Over the next four years, Roberts was essentially a squad player, fitting in wherever he was required across the back four. Upon the departure of Bobby McDonald in August 1980, Roberts came to the fore. Slotting into the, now vacant, right-back position, he became a first-team regular and was ever present during the 1980/81 season. Over the next three seasons, Roberts remained the first choice on the right side of the defence, becoming a key figure in the seemingly ever-constant battles for First Division survival.

December 1982 saw Roberts score his first goal for the Sky Blues after six years and 160 first-team games. Such a momentous occasion inspired the production of commemorative badges with the slogan 'I saw Harry score!' He scored a second the following month and jokingly suggested that he should move to centre forward. His scoring 'run', however, had come to an end, and they would be the only strikes in his time at Highfield Road.

In the mass exodus of first-team players during the close season of 1983, Roberts was one of the few to remain, and was appointed captain for the following season. His City career, however, was brought to an end during the spring of the campaign, when his surprise move to Birmingham City was announced. It brought to an end ten years with the Sky Blues, in which he had made 249 appearances. In recognition of his service, he was granted a testimonial later in the same year, in which a City past eleven played the current side in front of 3,000 supporters.

Roberts remained with the Blues for six seasons before moving to Wolves in 1990. He retired as a player in 1992. He later returned to Highfield Road to take up the position of youth development manager.

	League		FA Cup		League Cup		Total	
	Apps	Goals	Apps	Goals	Apps	Goals	Apps	Goals
1975/76	2	0	0	0	0	0	2	0
1976/77	12	0	1	0	0	0	13	0
1977/78	26	0	1	0	1 (1)	0	28 (1)	0
1978/79	17	0	0	0	0	0	17	0
1979/80	10(4)	0	0	0	2 (1)	0	12 (5)	0
1980/81	41(1)	0	4	0	9	0	54 (1)	0
1981/82	33(1)	0	1	0	2	0	36 (1)	0
1982/83	38	1	2	1	2	0	42	2
1983/84	30	0	4	0	3	0	37	0
TOTAL	209(6)	1	13	1	19(2)	0	241 (8)	2

Ted Roberts
Centre forward, 1937-52

Ted Roberts was yet another City player who was robbed of his best years by the Second World War. He was only twenty-one at the outbreak of hostilities and was just establishing himself at City after signing for the club in 1937. By the time of the resumption of domestic football, he was twenty-eight, and although he continued at City for a further six years, one wonders what 'may have been', had his career not been so severely interrupted.

Roberts was born in Chesterfield on 2 November 1916. He began his career with Glapwell Colliery, where he was spotted by Derby County. He signed for the Rams in 1934, remaining at the Baseball Ground for three years, before Harry Storer brought him to City. Roberts was signed, essentially, as cover for first-choice forwards, Jackie Brown, Leslie Jones and later Bill MacDonald, and until the war, he was primarily in the reserve side. However, whenever called upon he acquitted himself well, and made over 40 appearances before play was suspended.

During the war itself, Roberts only turned out twice for City, but when football restarted, he

became a regular up front and remained so for the next six seasons. He scored consistently, becoming renowned, in particular, for his ability in the air. His best haul came in 1948/49, when he netted 19 times, and by the time he left City in 1952, he had amassed a total of 87 goals, placing him third in the all-time list of City scorers.

His place up front had been threatened only once during this time, when, in late 1950, Tommy Briggs was signed from Grimsby Town. Briggs had scored prolifically for both of his previous clubs and was the intended replacement for Roberts who was, by now, in his mid-thirties. However, Roberts was only displaced for six games, the rumour being that his popularity with his team-mates led them to reject Briggs *en masse*, as a means of returning their man to the side.

Roberts eventually left Highfield Road in the close season of 1952, and moved into non-League football, first with Kings Lynn and, a year later, with Banbury Spencer. He returned in the late 1950s as assistant coach to Billy Frith, but became a victim of the King's Lynn cup defeat in 1961, which precipitated the sacking of the entire coaching staff. A fellow victim of the clearout was Roberts's former team-mate, Alf Wood.

	League		FA Cup		Total	
	Apps	Goals	Apps	Goals	Apps	Goals
1936/37	5	3	0	0	5	3
1937/38	23	6	1	0	24	6
1938/39	14	3	1	0	15	3
1946/47	29	9	2	1	31	10
1947/48	26	10	1	0	27	10
1948/49	34	19	1	0	35	19
1949/50	25	8	1	0	26	8
1950/51	31	15	1	0	32	15
1951/52	25	12	3	1	28	13
TOTAL	212	85	11	2	223	87

Nat Robinson
Goalkeeper, 1895-99 and 1910-15

Nat Robinson's long and distinguished career actually began with him playing as a half-back, the position for which he was signed by Singers in 1895. Robinson was seventeen at the time, and had been turning out for local side Allesley FC, when he was spotted by Singers and brought to Highfield Road. However, in a reserve team match against Foleshill St Lawrence in April 1895, he was forced to deputize between the posts after the first-choice 'keeper (and a number of other players) had failed to turn up for the match. By the end of the same season, he was turning out in goal for the first team, making his debut against West Bromwich reserves in February 1896, and by the following year, he had established himself as the regular first-choice 'keeper.

Over the next three years, Robinson missed only two matches for Singers, and was attracting attention from League clubs, such was his growing reputation. In 1899, he moved on to Small Heath, where he spent eight years in the first team. During this time, he helped the Birmingham club achieve promotion to the First Division in 1901, and was also called up on 2 occasions to represent the Football League team. In the close season of 1908, he moved on to Chelsea, and after two years at Stamford Bridge, he returned to Highfield Road to end his career with City.

In his second spell at Highfield Road, Robinson acted as deputy to Bob Evans, and, consequently, he played very few times for the first team. He made two appearances in January 1911, when Evans was injured, then announced his retirement from the game, becoming a local publican. However, his services were called upon once again in 1915, when City faced a crisis, due to the injury of 'keeper Sid Blake. Robinson stepped into the fray and made his final 5 appearances for City, almost nineteen years after first turning out for Singers.

| | Southern League | | FA Cup | | Total | |
	Apps	Goals	Apps	Goals	Apps	Goals
1910/11	1	0	1	0	2	0
1914/15	5	0	0	0	5	0
TOTAL	102	0	5	0	107	0

John Sillett
Right-back, 1962-66; manager 1986-90

John Sillett came to Coventry in April 1962, signed by Jimmy Hill from Chelsea, for a fee of £3,000. He had been at Stamford Bridge for eight years, playing alongside his brother, Peter, but had found himself unable to hold down a regular first-team place. He made his City debut in the penultimate game of the 1961/62 season and promptly became first choice at right-back. Over the next two seasons he missed only a handful of games as City won the Third Division championship. Injury problems, however, curtailed his opportunities in the Second Division and in 1966, he was transferred to Plymouth Argle.

After two years at Home Park, Sillett retired as a player and took up a coaching role at Bristol City. He spent six years at Ashton Gate before taking his first managerial post at Hereford United in 1974. Under Sillett the Bulls achieved promotion to the Second Division for the first time, earning him the 1975/76 Third Division Manager of the Year award. However, they were unable to consolidate and promptly returned to the Third. In early 1978, with Hereford languishing near the foot of the table, Sillett resigned.

In 1983, Sillett returned to Coventry as a coach under Bobby Gould. After falling out with Gould he left once again, only to return shortly after when Don Mackay took over as manager. By May 1986, Mackay too had left the manager's hotseat, and Sillett was asked to take over as chief coach in a managerial partnership with George Curtis.

Under Sillett and Curtis the team blossomed. Their refreshing approach tangibly improved team morale, and they were able to bring the best out of players who had hitherto underperformed. In May 1987, the duo led City to their historic FA Cup win, and Coventry's first major trophy. After the Cup Final, Sillett became sole manager and strove to build on the success. In his three years at the helm, Coventry enjoyed relative prosperity, and although never Championship contenders, spent more time than not in the top half of the table. A testimony to Sillett is that in his reign as manager, City were never involved in a relegation battle.

Ironically, the FA Cup provided the major stains on Sillett's management record at Highfield Road. The third round exits to Sutton and Northampton were an embarrassment he struggled to live down. In October 1990, after indicating he would not extend his contract, Sillett was sacked, being replaced by Terry Butcher. After leaving City, he returned to Edgar Street for a second spell as Hereford manager.

| | League | | FA Cup | | League Cup | | | Total | |
	Apps	Goals	Apps	Goals	Apps	Goals		Apps	Goals
1961/62	2	0	0	0	0	0		2	0
1962/63	38	1	9	0	2	0		49	1
1963/64	41	0	2	0	2	1		45	1
1964/65	17	0	1	0	3	0		21	0
1965/66	10(1)	0	0	0	0	0		10(1)	0
TOTAL	108(1)	1	12	0	7	1		127(1)	2

Noel Simpson
Left half, 1948-57

Born and bred in Nottinghamshire, Noel Simpson began his playing career during the war, turning out for both Nottingham clubs' wartime sides, before signing up with Forest in 1943. When football restarted in 1946, Simpson was a regular for Forest, spending two seasons at the City Ground before transferring to Coventry for £8,000 in August 1948. He made his debut on the opening day of the 1948/49 season in the 2-2 draw away at Brentford, starting a City career which lasted nine seasons and 270 appearances.

Simpson was a model of consistency in the City side during a time of rapid player turnover and significant change, as the club sought to recreate to successful pre-war era. Such was the regularity of change at the club, that Simpson found himself playing under seven different managers in his time at Highfield Road! Throughout, Simpson maintained his place at the left side of the defence, overcoming elongated periods of injury in 1951 and 1953. At the start of the 1954/55 season, City manager Jack Fairbrother appointed Simpson as club captain, an honour he held for two seasons.

In time for the 1956/57 season, Harry Warren was appointed as City's new manager, a move which would signal the end of Simpson's playing days at Highfield Road. Warren made major changes in his attempt to turn around the club's fortunes, and in January of 1957, after a 4-2 drubbing by Colchester, he switched Iain Jamieson from right to left half, replacing Simpson. By this stage, Simpson was thirty-four, and never regained his place in the side. He was allowed to leave at the end of the campaign, to finish his career on the South Coast with Exeter City. He spent only a year at St James's Park, making 33 appearances, before retiring from the game and returning to Nottinghamshire.

| | League | | FA Cup | | Total | |
	Apps	Goals	Apps	Goals	Apps	Goals
1948/49	33	1	0	0	33	1
1949/50	38	1	1	0	39	1
1950/51	16	2	0	0	16	2
1951/52	35	1	3	0	38	1
1952/53	33	1	3	0	36	1
1953/54	18	0	0	0	18	0
1954/55	25	0	4	0	29	0
1955/56	37	1	1	0	38	1
1956/57	23	0	0	0	23	0
TOTAL	258	7	12	0	270	7

Billy Smith

Forward, 1907-08, 1909-12 and 1913-14

Billy Smith was a natural goalscorer, who had three separate spells with Coventry during the late Birmingham League and early Southern League eras. Born in 1882, Smith began his playing career with West Bromwich Baptists, where he quickly gained a reputation as a strong and talented centre forward. His prolific goalscoring, which included a note-worthy double hat-trick against Halesowen, quickly attracted the attention of bigger clubs and, after a brief spell with Worcester City, he joined West Bromwich Albion in 1902. He spent five years at the Hawthorns, before Alderman Fred Lee signed Smith for his first spell at City in 1907.

In his first season at City, Smith was a sensation. His 33 League goals in as many games helped Coventry to their highest ever position of fourth in the Birmingham League. In the FA Cup, Smith added a further 5 goals as City reached the first round proper for the first time in their history. However, due to an administrative oversight, which was branded as 'incompetence', Coventry failed to re-sign Smith at the end of the season, and he left to join Small Heath.

After a year with the Birmingham club, he returned to Highfield Road in time for the 1909/10 season. His second term at City lasted for three seasons and coincided with a successful period for the side, as they consolidated their position in the Southern League and also embarked on a famous FA Cup run, which saw them reach the quarter-finals. Smith played more of a supporting role to the front line during this time, turning provider for players such as Harry Buckle and Fred Jones. Nevertheless, he still managed to convert 26 goals himself over the course of his three seasons, including one in the 3-1 cup win over First Division side, Nottingham Forest, which heralded the last-eight showdown with Everton in 1910.

Smith left Highfield Road in 1912 to spend a season with Nuneaton Town, but returned in 1913 for a final year with the Bantams. However, by this stage he was past his best and showed only glimpses of the talent that had made him such a firm favourite with the City fans. In a poor season, which saw City relegated to the Second Division of the Southern League, Smith played 15 games to bring his total appearances for City to 130. In the summer of 1914, he finally left Highfield Road for good, retiring from the game aged thirty.

| | Birmingham League | | FA Cup | | | Total | |
	Apps	Goals	Apps	Goals		Apps	Goals
1907/08	33	33	9	5		42	38

| | Southern League | | FA Cup | | | Total | |
	Apps	Goals	Apps	Goals		Apps	Goals
1909/10	22	8	4	1		26	9
1910/11	23	7	4	1		27	8
1911/12	18	9	2	0		20	9
1913/14	15	0	0	0		15	0
TOTAL	111	57	19	7		130	64

David Speedie
Forward, 1987-91

David Speedie was John Sillett's major acquisition with the funds of the 1987 FA Cup final success, signing for a club record £780,000 in the close season of that year. Speedie had begun his League career with Barnsley, after being turned down by both Doncaster and Everton for being 'too small'. However, after finding himself unable to hold down a first-team place with the Tykes, he moved on to Darlington in June 1980. He spent two years at Feethams and in his final season, 1981/82, he headed the club's scoring charts, netting 17 times. It was this form which alerted the attention of Chelsea and in the close season of 1982, he signed for the Stamford Bridge club for a fee of £70,000.

After five years at Stamford Bridge he joined the Sky Blues, making an immediate impact by netting in his debut in the opening game of the 1987/88 season. Making this even sweeter was the fact that the opponents that day were City's FA Cup adversaries of three months previously, Tottenham Hotspur. Speedie became a firm favourite with the City fans, with his dynamic displays and his obvious commitment in every match. He scored some exquisite goals during his time at Highfield Road, including a number of inch-perfect chipped goals, which became something of a trademark. In 1988/89, he headed the club's scoring charts with 15 goals and, in total, amassed a sum of 35 during his four years at City.

Speedie's international career was, undoubtedly, hampered by his disciplinary problems, however, he added a further 5 caps whilst with Coventry to the solitary cap he won whilst at Chelsea. In total, he would win 10 caps for Scotland.

Speedie's fiery temperament was indicative of the passion with which he embraced the game; on a number of occasions this led to disciplinary problems. Shortly after the arrival of Terry Butcher at Highfield Road, an off-field incident involving one of the club's vice-presidents precipitated his departure from Highfield Road. In January 1991, a fee of £700,000 saw Speedie transfer to Liverpool, for whom he made a mere 12 League appearances, prior to joining Blackburn Rovers in August of the same year. After eleven months at Ewood Park, Speedie transferred to Southampton, and after loan periods at Birmingham, West Brom and West Ham during 1992/93, he joined Leicester in 1993, where he finished his League career.

	League		FA Cup		League Cup		Other		Total	
	Apps	Goals	Apps	Goals	Apps	Goals	Apps	Goals	Apps	Goals
1987/88	35 (1)	6	1 (1)	0	2	0	2	1	40 (2)	7
1988/89	36	14	1	0	3	1	1	0	41	15
1989/90	32	8	1	0	7	1	0	0	40	9
1990/91	18	3	0	0	3	1	0	0	21	4
TOTAL	121 (1)	31	3 (1)	0	15	3	3	1	142 (2)	35

Colin Stein
Centre forward, 1972-75

By the time of his arrival at Highfield Road, Colin Stein was already an established Scottish international with a proven goalscoring record at club level. He had begun his League career with Hibernian, signing for the Edinburgh club from non-League Armadale Thistle for £200. At the time, he was a raw eighteen-year-old striker, but in his three years at Easter Road, he matured into a dynamic frontman with a keen eye for goal. In 1968, he transferred to Rangers in a deal which saw him become the first six-figure transfer between two Scottish clubs and began a highly-successful four years at Ibrox. In November of the same year, he achieved the incredible feat of scoring a hat-trick in just three minutes against Arbroath, instantly endearing himself to the Rangers faithful. He was part of the team which won the Scottish League Cup and were runners-up in the Scottish FA Cup in 1971 and, a year later, scored in the 3-2 triumph over Dynamo Kiev, which captured the European Cup-winners' Cup for the Glaswegians. By this stage, he had already established himself on the international scene after making his Scottish debut in a thrilling 5-3 away win over Wales in 1969.

Stein's transfer to Coventry was as much of a shock to the Rangers supporters as it was a coup for the Sky Blues. The deal which brought him to Highfield Road had seen Quinton Young make the opposite trip, and a further £100,000 being paid to Rangers. He made an immediate impact, adding the necessary impetus required to lift City from a precarious position in the relegation zone. Alongside fellow Scot, Tommy Hutchison, he added a degree of sparkle to the side (which had been lacking) and quickly became a crowd favourite with his all-action displays. Towards the end of his first year at City, he also won what were to be his final four caps for Scotland, bringing his career tally to 21.

Over the next two seasons, Stein continued to impress with his all-round performances, despite the fact that his scoring rate dropped somewhat, netting just 10 times in 1973/74, and 7 in 1974/75 up until his sale in March. His departure from Highfield Road was precipitated by the financial crisis sparked by the signing of Larry Lloyd the previous autumn, which had left the club needing to dispense with some of their most valued assets in order to remain solvent. With £80,000 on offer from Rangers, City were in no position to refuse, and the Scot returned to Ibrox after just 98 games for the Sky Blues. The move was part of a double blow to City fans, who were also to see Willie Carr depart in the same month, with further sacrifices imminent.

Just two months after his return to Rangers, Stein scored the goal which clinched the Scottish League Championship after nine consecutive years of triumph by their archrivals, Celtic. He won a League Cup winners' medal the following year, although his career was on the wane by this point, and he never managed to recapture the form of his first spell at Ibrox. In October 1977, he was loaned out for a spell at Kilmarnock, and in the close season of 1978, he announced his retirement after 206 games for the Gers.

	League		FA Cup		League Cup		Total	
	Apps	Goals	Apps	Goals	Apps	Goals	Apps	Goals
1972/73	31	10	4	2	0	0	35	12
1973/74	28	6	2	0	6	4	36	10
1974/75	24	6	2	0	1	1	27	7
TOTAL	83	22	8	2	7	5	98	29

Ray Straw
Centre forward, 1957-61

Born in Ilkeston, Derbyshire on 22 May 1933, Ray Straw began his playing days with non-league side Ilkeston Town, whilst working in the local coal mine. His brother, Eric, was also a keen footballer and had trials with Leeds United, but it was Ray who would go on to make the grade in professional football and in October 1951 he signed for Derby County. Straw found his chances for first-team action in the First Division severely limited, however, he was given his chance once Derby has suffered relegation to the Third Division (North), and he proved a revelation. Equally able to strike with either foot, Straw was prolific in his final years at the Baseball Ground scoring 57 goals in 97 matches, including a club record 37 in 1956/57; a record which stands to this day. Straw left the Baseball in November 1957 to become Billy Frith's first signing upon his taking over the managerial position at Coventry for the second time.

The agenda for Coventry at this crucial time was clear: they had to avoid finishing in the bottom half of the Third Division (South) in order that they would not become founder members of the new Fourth Division when the leagues were reorganised in time for the 1958/59 season. The signing of Straw was part of Frith's plan to breathe new life into the side and lift them to the safety of the division's upper half

He made his City debut in the 4-1 defeat against Millwall on 23 November 1957. It was the first in a series of four straight defeats, the worst of possible starts for the new signing. Straw gradually settled into the side and began to find his scoring touch. Hat-tricks against Walsall and Shrewsbury helped Straw to 14 goals in his first season; however, it was not enough to prevent City finishing nineteenth, and life in the Fourth loomed.

Coventry were destined to remain in the Fourth Division for one solitary season, with the Straw's goalscoring being a major factor in the turnaround in the club's fortunes. He was a sensation in 1958/59, a formidable striking force who gave the long-suffering fans the new hero that they had so longed for. He netted 30 goals, including a memorable hat-trick in the 7-1 defeat of Aldershot. Coventry finished the season second behind Port Vale and were promoted to the Third Division in time for the dawn of the 1960s.

The opening game of the following season saw Straw become the first player to have played in every one of the Football League's six divisions and, fittingly, he marked the occasion with a goal in the 2-0 victory over Mansfield Town. His dynamic form continued as Coventry looked for so long like contenders for a second consecutive promotion. In all he scored 21 goals, including a hat-trick in the 4-2 win over Mansfield in April 1960. Unfortunately, their promotion push fizzled out in the final weeks of the season and City finished in fourth place.

1960/61 was to be Straw's final season with City. In a disappointing season in which Coventry finished only fifteenth in the Third, Straw's goals proved to be one of few bright points. He again top-scored with 20 goals, to bring his overall tally in his four years at Highfield Road to 85. His remains a goalscoring record unsurpassed in post-war City history, made all the more impressive given that it was achieved in such a short time span.

It was somewhat of a surprise when it was announced in August 1961 that he had been sold to Mansfield Town. It was to be his final league club, where he remained for two seasons. In all he made 50 appearances for the Stags, scoring 14 goals, and helping them to promotion to the Third Division in 1962/63, his final season. After retiring from league football, he continued playing with non-league Lockheed Leamington, before returning to live in his native Ilkeston, where he remained until his death in 2001.

	League		FA Cup		League Cup		Total	
	Apps	Goals	Apps	Goals	Apps	Goals	Apps	Goals
1957/58	22	14	1	0	-	-	23	14
1958/59	44	27	2	3	-	-	46	30
1959/60	43	20	2	1	-	-	45	21
1960/61	33	18	3	2	1	0	37	20
TOTAL	142	79	8	6	1	0	151	85

Ray Straw in action against Reading.

Danny Thomas
Right-back, 1978-83

Danny Thomas was, undoubtedly, one of the brightest talents to emerge from City's youth policy in the late 1970s and early '80s. Prior to joining City, he had trials with both Leeds and Sheffield United, but elected to come to Highfield Road as an apprentice. His elder brother, Val, was also on the City books, but it was Danny who was to make the grade and break through into the first team. Thomas matured quickly and made his first-team debut at the age of seventeen, in the League Cup tie with West Brom in September 1979. His League debut followed just three days later, as a substitute in the draw with Tottenham Hotspur, although he would wait until the following season for his first League start for City. Initially a midfielder, Thomas switched to what would become his customary right-back role after coming on as a substitute in the away match at Aston Villa in 1980/81, clearly displaying natural attributes as a full-back. He made the position his own during the latter half of the same season and won the accolade of City Player of the Year for 1980/81. The following season, Thomas missed only 3 matches through injury and, alongside his second consecutive City Player of the Year award, was also named as Midland Player of the Season.

International recognition came after less than 20 first-class appearances for Thomas, when he was selected to play for the England under-21s. In total, he made 5 appearances at this level, before graduating to the senior squad in November 1982. Thomas was somewhat unfortunate that, at the time, Phil Neal was well established in the right-back role for England, and thus his international opportunities were limited. His full international debut came in July 1983 on the summer tour to Australia, where he played in 2 matches against the host country. They proved to be his only full England appearances.

Shortly after his return from this tour, he left City and joined Spurs for £300,000. His time at Spurs was limited by a serious injury sustained in March 1987, which forced his retirement from the game at the age of only twenty-six. Had it not been for this unfortunate incident, Thomas could well have lined up against City in the FA Cup final later that year. Following his retirement, he trained as a physiotherapist, returning to the game as physiotherapist to Ossie Ardiles' West Brom team.

	League		FA Cup		League Cup		Total	
	Apps	Goals	Apps	Goals	Apps	Goals	Apps	Goals
1979/80	0 (3)	0	0	0	1	0	1 (3)	0
1980/81	23 (2)	1	2 (1)	1	5 (1)	0	30 (4)	2
1981/82	39	1	4	0	2	0	45	1
1982/83	41	3	3	0	3	0	47	3
TOTAL	103 (5)	5	9 (1)	1	11 (1)	0	123 (7)	6

Garry Thompson
Centre forward, 1977-83

Garry Thompson was one of a crop of exciting youngsters to emerge from the City youth system in the late 1970s. A tall and powerful striker, he possessed excellent heading ability and explosive pace. After signing as a professional in June 1977, he got his initial first-team opportunity in 1977/78, deputizing for the injury-prone Mick Ferguson. Thompson equipped himself admirably, and was beginning to establish himself when he suffered a broken leg in a training accident in March 1979; an injury that was to keep him out of contention for almost a year.

In early 1980, Thompson returned from injury better than ever, fitting seamlessly back into the City forward line. In 1980/81, he enjoyed his most prolific season for City, netting 15 goals and earning a call-up to the England under-21 team. He featured heavily in the memorable League Cup run, scoring 6 as City almost reached their first major final. In the first leg of the semi-final against West Ham, Thompson had the unfortunate distinction of scoring the opener for the opposition, before redeeming himself with two strikes in City's fightback, which eventually saw them triumph 3-2. Unfortunately, the Hammers proved too strong in the second leg, and City eventually bowed out 4-3 on aggregate.

Thompson remained with City for two further years, during which time he increased his goal tally to 49 in 158 games. In February 1983, the decision was taken to sell Thompson, who was at this stage a valuable asset. It was widely reported that his sale was at the behest of the chairman, Jimmy Hill, who took the decision out of the hands of team manager, Dave Sexton. Thompson's sale to West Bromwich Albion earned City £225,000, but resulted in a great deal of resentment from Sexton, who was increasingly out of tune with the board, and was eventually sacked at the end of the season.

In his two years with the Baggies, Thompson continued to score with regularity, and his value had doubled by the time of his sale to Sheffield Wednesday in August 1985. There then began a series of moves, with Thompson never remaining at any club for more than two years. Over the course of the late 1980s and early '90s, he moved on to Aston Villa, Watford, Crystal Palace, Queens Park Rangers, and Cardiff City, before bringing his career to a close with Northampton Town.

	League		FA Cup		League Cup			Total	
	Apps	Goals	Apps	Goals	Apps	Goals		Apps	Goals
1977/78	5 (1)	2	0	0	0	0		5 (1)	2
1978/79	19 (1)	8	2	0	0 (1)	1		21 (2)	9
1979/80	16 (1)	6	0	0	0	0		16 (1)	6
1980/81	34 (1)	8	4	1	7	6		45 (1)	15
1981/82	35 (1)	10	3	2	2	0		40 (1)	12
1982/83	18 (2)	4	2	1	3	0		23 (2)	5
TOTAL	127 (7)	38	11	4	12 (1)	7		150 (8)	49

Charlie Timmins
Right-back, 1946-58

Charlie Timmins joined Coventry City immediately after the Second World War, signing from amateur side, Jack Moulds Athletic. He was twenty-four at the time of his arrival, but spent three years in the reserve side, before finally making his debut in August 1949, at the relatively late age of twenty-seven. Over the next nine years, Timmins proved himself to be a most loyal servant of the club, and a solid, dependable full-back, who would go on to over 160 appearances for the Bantams.

After making his debut at the start of the 1949/50 season, Timmins battled with Martin McDonnell for the regular right-back spot, with the pair sharing the position throughout the campaign. The following year, however, McDonnell converted to a central defensive position, and Timmins was able to establish himself as the number one in his position at the right side of the defensive line. He was troubled by a number of injuries during the early 1950s and struggled to regain his place in the first team, facing increased competition not only from McDonnell, who had reverted back to full-back in 1952, but also from Ken Jones and, later, Frank Austin. Consequently, Timmins featured only periodically in the side during the mid-1950s. In 1957, he was appointed as club captain, and enjoyed a spell at left-back, before bringing his career at City to an end in the close season of 1958. After leaving City, he dropped into non-League football with local side Lockheed Leamington.

	League		FA Cup		Total	
	Apps	Goals	Apps	Goals	Apps	Goals
1949/50	23	0	0	0	23	0
1950/51	33	0	1	0	34	0
1951/52	7	0	0	0	7	0
1952/53	11	0	0	0	11	0
1953/54	16	0	0	0	16	0
1954/55	9	1	0	0	9	1
1955/56	19	2	1	0	20	2
1956/57	23	1	1	0	24	1
1957/58	20	1	1	0	21	1
TOTAL	161	5	4	0	165	5

Ian Wallace
Forward, 1976-80

Upon signing the unknown Scot Ian Wallace, Coventry manager Gordon Milne made the prediction that the flame-haired striker would 'set Highfield Road alight'. Over the next four years, Wallace proved Milne's words to be prophetic, as he established himself as City's most prolific goalscorer of the decade. His dynamic and aggressive style of play made him a firm favourite with the fans from the outset, and his partnership with Mick Ferguson remains arguably the most exciting strike pairing of City's top flight era.

Wallace cost City a mere £40,000 when signed from Dumbaton in August 1976. His time at Coventry, however, got off to the worst possible of starts, when, after only 6 games, he was involved in a horrific car accident, which almost cost him his sight. He recovered to play 26 games in his debut season, scoring 9 times as City struggled against relegation.

The following season, Wallace spearheaded one of City's most exciting teams of the top flight era, as they pushed for a European place. His formidable partnership with Mick Ferguson blossomed, with the pair between them accounting for more than half of City's record 75 First Division goals. Wallace himself became the only Coventry player to date to score over 20 League goals in a season since the club reached the top flight, netting 21 times. His performances earned him his first international call-up, making a scoring debut for Scotland in the 2-1 win over Bulgaria in February 1978. During his time at City, he would appear in a further 2 internationals for the Scots.

Wallace remained with the club for a further two seasons. However, by the latter half of 1979/80, he appeared increasingly unsettled and had been dropped to the reserves. When Brian Clough offered £1.25 million for the striker in the close season of 1980, City gratefully accepted and Wallace was on his way to the City Ground.

After leaving Highfield Road, Wallace never regained the prolific form that had seen him become one of the country's top marksmen whilst with Coventry. After four years at Nottingham, he transferred to the continent with Dutch club, Brest, returning for a brief spell with Sunderland in 1985, before travelling again, first to Portugal and then to Australia.

	League		FA Cup		League Cup		Total	
	Apps	Goals	Apps	Goals	Apps	Goals	Apps	Goals
1976/77	24 (2)	9	0	0	0	0	24 (2)	9
1977/78	41	21	1	0	4	2	46	23
1978/79	38	15	2	0	1	0	41	15
1979/80	25	13	1	0	1	0	27	13
TOTAL	128 (2)	58	4	0	6	2	138 (2)	60

Ian Wallace.

Leslie 'Plum' Warner
Outside right, 1937-54

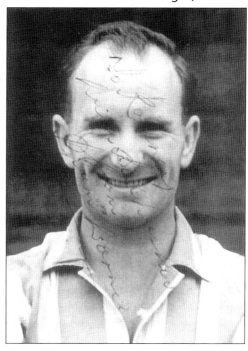

Les Warner began his career with Shirley Juniors and Jack Moulds Athletic, before signing for City in September 1937. Known as 'Plum' after the famous cricketer, Sir Pelham Warner, he spent many of the pre-war years in City's reserves, kept out of the first team due to the consistency of George Taylor on the right flank. He did, however, make 8 appearances before the war, including a memorable debut against Swansea in February 1938. Coventry won the match 5-0, with Warner creating each of the goals. At the end of the match, the crowd invaded the pitch and 'chaired' Warner back to the dressing room.

During the war, Warner's appearances for City were limited to 46, as a result of his army service. He also played for Watford during hostilities as a guest. In the first two post-war seasons, Warner vied with Dennis Simpson for the position of outside right, before making the spot his own in the 1948/49 season. Over the next five years, he was Coventry's first choice on the right flank, delighting with his exciting wing play, if infuriating at times, due to over-elaboration. His best seasons came in 1950/51, when City finished seventh in the Second Division, and the 1952/53 promotion challenge from Division Three (South). It was a cruel blow for City when Warner was sidelined with injury in the promotion run-in of 1953, when the team faltered in the final games to finish sixth.

By the start of 1953/4, the young Gordon Nutt had emerged and taken over the right-wing spot from Warner. In his final season, Warner made only 3 appearances, as Nutt established himself in the side. Consequently, he decided to bring an end to seventeen years at City, retiring in the close season of 1954, after 207 games for Coventry. He remained in the city until the time of his death in 1982.

	League		FA Cup		Total	
	Apps	Goals	Apps	Goals	Apps	Goals
1937/38	2	0	0	0	2	0
1938/39	4	0	0	0	4	0
1945/46	-	-	2	0	2	0
1946/47	16	0	0	0	16	0
1947/48	7	3	2	2	9	5
1948/49	29	3	1	0	30	3
1949/50	30	3	1	0	31	3
1950/51	41	4	1	0	42	4
1951/52	31	1	0	0	31	1
1952/53	34	5	3	1	37	6
1953/54	3	0	0	0	3	0
TOTAL	197	19	10	3	207	22

Alf Wood
Goalkeeper, 1935-51 & 1955-59

Alf Wood holds the record of being the oldest player to have played a first-class game for Coventry, when in 1958 he came out of retirement to cover for injury at the age of 44. His City career began some twenty-three years earlier, when he signed for Harry Storer's City as a twenty year old, from Nuneaton Town. With Bill Morgan incumbent in the City goal, however, Wood's chances of first-team action were limited; his debut in the February 1938 victory over Swansea Town being one of only two pre-war appearances.

Wood came into his own during the war, making 96 wartime appearances and guesting for Northampton Town, all despite the setback of a bout of spinal meningitis, which almost ended his career. Upon the cessation of hostilities, Wood embarked on a consecutive run of 216 league and cup games, lasting through until 1951. He eventually lost his place in the City goal in October 1951, ousted by Peter Taylor. Aged 36, he finally left Highfield Road to join Northampton in a deal worth £2,100.

After 139 appearances for Northampton, Wood returned to City as player-coach in 1955. Deputising for the injured Reg Matthews, he played four games in 1956 before officially 'retiring' as a player. However in September 1958, regular 'keeper Jim Sanders broke his ankle, and with deputy Graham Spratt considered too much of a risk, Wood was called upon once more to guard the City net. He played a further twelve matches, seven of which were victories, including four clean sheets. Wood remained as a coach with City until the fateful FA Cup defeat against Kings Lynn in November 1961. The defeat cost not only manager Billy Frith his job, but also the entire coaching staff, including Wood. Clearly bitter about his sacking, he was quoted at the time as saying 'We are the victims of the results, but we have been trying to teach carthorses to be footballers.' It was an unfortunate end to an illustrious association with City which had lasted almost 36 years. After leaving Coventry, Wood briefly managed Walsall, before retiring from football altogether.

	League Apps	Goals	FA Cup Apps	Goals	Total Apps	Goals
1937/38	1	0	0	0	1	0
1938/39	1	0	0	0	1	0
1945/46	WW2		2	0	2	0
1946/47	42	0	2	0	44	0
1947/48	42	0	2	0	44	0
1948/49	42	0	1	0	43	0
1949/50	42	0	1	0	43	0
1950/51	41	0	1	0	42	0
1951/52	10	0	0	0	10	0
1955/56	1	0	0	0	1	0
1956/57	2	0	1	0	3	0
1958/59	10	0	2	0	12	0
TOTAL	234	0	12	0	246	0

Billy Yates
Right half 1911-14,

Billy Yates was much travelled by the time he arrived at City in June 1911. Born in Birmingham, he began playing for Erdington where he was scouted by Aston Villa, signing at Villa Park as a nineteen-year-old in March 1903. In his two years with the Aston club, he never managed to make the breakthrough into their League side, and consequently moved south to join Brighton and Hove Albion in 1905. He remained on the South Coast for just one year, before transferring to Manchester United in the close season of 1906. Again he moved on after just one season, leaving Old Trafford to play north of the Border with Hearts. He became the first Englishman to play in a Scottish Cup Final, emerging with a runners-up medal, before switching to Portsmouth in the summer of 1908. It was while at Pompey that he made the switch from inside forward to half-back, the position he would fill so successfully at Highfield Road. At Fratton Park, he was a regular for three seasons before joining his final club, Coventry City, in June 1911.

Yates was thrust into the side for the opening day of the 1911/12 season, and quickly proved to be a valuable addition to the team. He was a sturdy and consistent right half, whose work rate was second to none. He was also noted as a good reader of the game, showing the ability to anticipate opposition moves to make early decisive tackles. Throughout his first two seasons at City, he was ever present, completing over 100 consecutive games before he missed his first match for the club in January 1914. He was appointed as club captain in time for the 1913/14 season, his last for the club, and he had the unfortunate 'honour' of presiding over the campaign where City were relegated from the Southern League's First Division. At the end of the season, Yates brought an end to his playing career, after 111 matches for City in just three years. He was thirty-one at the time, but left the game altogether to become a publican.

| | Southern League | | FA Cup | | Total | |
	Apps	Goals	Apps	Goals	Apps	Goals
1911/12	38	0	2	0	40	0
1912/13	38	1	2	0	40	1
1913/14	30	0	1	0	31	0
TOTAL	106	1	5	0	111	1

Terry Yorath
Midfield, 1976-79

By the time of his arrival at Coventry in August 1976, Terry Yorath was an established Welsh international who had earned a League Championship winners medal, two European runners-up medals and an FA cup runners-up medal with Leeds United. His experience was something Gordon Milne identified was clearly lacking from the City midfield, and, at the peak of his career, his signing for £125,000 was an astute move by the City manager. Yorath was a tough-tackling, no nonsense midfielder, and quickly became a pivotal figure at the heart of City's team. Appointed captain on his arrival, he oversaw the transformation from the relegation-threatened side of 1976/77 to the exciting European chasing team of the following season. His personal performances, particularly in 1977/78, were outstanding, and his leadership of the team was a crucial element in the development of the side.

Yorath began his career at Elland Road, signing professional forms as a seventeen year old in April 1967. Consigned to the fringes of the Leeds side during the late 1960s, he gradually established himself and played a significant role in the League Championship-winning side of 1973/74. From 1970 he was a regular for the Welsh national side, making 28 appearances and earning the captaincy whilst with Leeds.

His Coventry debut came in the 3-1 defeat at the hands of Liverpool in September 1976. During his first season at the club, Coventry battled relegation, with Yorath's leadership from the middle contributing much to their eventual survival. During 1977/78, Yorath played in all but two matches, as the team developed into an exciting, attacking forced. His midfield partnership with Barry Powell in the attacking 4-2-4 formation played a major part in the success of the team, in what was one of the most exciting campaigns of the top-flight era. Injuries hampered Yorath during 1978/79, limiting his appearances to twenty-one games.

In August 1979, he left City for Tottenham Hotspur in a deal worth £275,000, citing a desire to win honours as his rationale. He remained at White Hart Lane for two years before joining Canadian club Vancouver Whitecaps in 1981. A year later he returned to England with Bradford City, where he stayed until joining Swansea City as player manager in 1986.

In 1987, Yorath retired as a player and concentrated on developing a career in management. Since this time he has had two spells in charge at Swansea City, divided by a year as manager at Bradford City, and he has also managed the Welsh national side. From a Coventry perspective, it is interesting to consider how his management career might have developed had he accepted Don Mackay's invitation to become his assistant manager in 1986.

	League		FA Cup		League Cup			Total	
	Apps	Goals	Apps	Goals	Apps	Goals		Apps	Goals
1976/77	38	1	1	0	3	0		42	1
1977/78	40	2	1	0	3	0		44	2
1978/79	21	0	0	0	0	0		21	0
TOTAL	99	3	2	0	6	0		107	3